THE A-Z OF HANDICRAFTS

THE A-Z OF HANDICRAFTS

OCTOPUS

First published in 1976 by Octopus Books Limited
59 Grosvenor Street, London W.1.

© 1976 Octopus Books Limited

ISBN 0 7064 0540 4

Produced by Mandarin Publishers Limited
22a Westlands Road, Quarry Bay, Hong Kong
Printed in Hong Kong

INTRODUCTION

Over the last decade or so, handicraft pursuits have enjoyed an enormous upsurge in popularity. Traditional handicrafts, such as patchwork and quilting, tie-dyeing and batik, beadwork and embroidery of all sorts – the origins and history of which in many cases, are lost in antiquity – have shot back into fashion, whilst new 'handicrafts' have emerged to meet the demands of contemporary living. All have been greatly enriched by the introduction of modern fabrics, colours and designs, which have done much to make handicrafts more exciting. Economy has doubtless had much to do with the current popularity. Clothes, gifts and all manner of household items, nursery and garden accessories – many examples of which will be found on the following pages – can be made at home at a fraction of the cost of an equivalent shop-bought item. They have the advantage that they may be made in the sort of materials wanted to achieve a chosen effect.

This book sets out many well-known, and some lesser known, handicrafts in an easy-to-follow A–Z sequence. The techniques of the crafts are explained and patterns relating specifically to each one are given. The traditional handicrafts already mentioned are present with some exciting and unusual ways of using them, and recently popularized crafts, such as candle and collage making, and constructing mobiles and wall hangings – now so much part of home decor – are also included. There are some enchanting patterns for making economical toys and some bright knitting, crochet and rug-making patterns, to name only a few. In addition there is a store of practical advice on the use and handling of different types of materials, including paper, leather, suede and felt. Techniques for appliqué work and smocking are fully explained; there are detailed instructions for how to work a wealth of embroidery stitches and a simple explanation of how to make paper patterns, as well as transferring designs to fabric, proves just how easy these really are to do. Happily, the days are gone when handicraft pursuits were pastimes only for those people who were especially talented or had lots of spare time. Nowadays, anybody can try their hand at any number of different crafts, and this book will help to ensure success.

Metrication
Imperial measurements have been used in all patterns throughout this book. The metric equivalents are:
1 in. = 2·5 cm.
1 ft = 30 cm.
1 yd = 90 cm.

Abbreviations
The following abbreviations are the ones used in the knitting and crochet patterns contained in this book. Where it has been necessary to include additional abbreviations to cover specific points, these are given and explained at the beginning of the pattern to which they apply.

Knitting
k.	knit
p.	purl
g.st.	garter stitch
st.st.	stocking stitch
st(s).	stitch(es)
inc.	increase
dec.	decrease
alt.	alternate
foll.	following

beg.	beginning
cont.	continue
patt.	pattern
tog.	together
p.u.k.	pick up loop lying before next st. and k. into back of it
rep.	repeat
rem.	remaining
p.s.s.o.	pass slipped st. over
sl.	slip
t.b.l.	through back of loops
d.m.st.	double moss stitch
m.st.	moss stitch
s.k.p.o.	slip 1, knit 1, pass slipped stitch over
k.b.l. or p.b.l.	knit or purl into back of next stitch
w. or y.r.n.	wool or yarn round needle
* asterisk	repeat instructions following the asterisks as many times as specified in addition to the original

Crochet
As some crochet terminology is different to the American, the American equivalents follow afterwards in parentheses.

ch.	chain

d.c.	double crochet
(s.c.)	(single crochet)
hlf tr.	half treble
(h.d.c.)	(half double)
tr.	treble
(d.c.)	(double)
sp(s).	space(s)
st(s).	stitch(s)
s.s.	slip stitch
sp(s).	space(s) = 2ch., miss 2ch. or tr., 1tr. into next ch. or tr.
blk(s).	block(s) = 4tr., plus 3tr. for each additional block in group
* asterisk	repeat instructions following the asterisks as many more times as specified in addition to the original
( )	repeat instructions in parentheses as many times as specified

Needles
Knitting needles and crochet hook sizes have been given in this book in British standard sizes. American equivalents follow immediately afterwards in parentheses. American equivalent terms are given in parentheses after British terms.

ADHESIVES

Adhesives are widely used in all sorts of handicrafts work particularly in such fields as woodwork, papier mâché and some forms of jewellery making. They can however, also be very useful in handicrafts that involve the use of fabric mainly, or even exclusively. Motifs or appliqués can, in some cases be stuck onto a background instead of sewn, articles can be trimmed with braid and finishes that are glued in place, pictures can be created wholly by sticking pieces of fabrics onto a piece of card or other material to make an attractive design, and even complete garments can be made by gluing seams instead of sewing them.

The most important thing when using adhesives is to select the right one to suit the fabric involved and the purpose for which the finished article is needed. When making garments for example, it is best to choose materials which do not fray too badly and to use a specially recommended fabric adhesive. These are usually rubber-latex based and will withstand washing – although not dry cleaning – and ironing with a cool iron. (This also means of course, that you must use washable material.) Manufacturers of such adhesive also supply a special 'remover' to remove spilt or excess glue from fabric without marking it. In spite of this, it is better to use the glue sparingly in the first instance!

A rubber cement adhesive is ideal for glueing leather as it neither stiffens the material, nor penetrates it too deeply. It will also rub off easily if necessary, and may be thinned with cellulose thinner if it becomes too thick and hard. For making pictures, where you may be using a variety of fabrics and perhaps other materials, you may need to use several different adhesives. For heavier fabrics and most trimmings, use one of the recommended fabric adhesives, and for lightweight fabrics and paper, wallpaper paste used sparingly is ideal. If you are including hard, irregular shaped objects which do not necessarily have a flat surface but need a firm bond, use a clear all-purpose adhesive. Arrange all the components of your picture before

applying adhesive to anything so that you know in advance exactly where you want everything to go. Apply adhesive sparingly and begin by sticking down the background and larger shapes first, filling in the smaller details afterwards. Double-sided adhesive tape can be very useful in picture making, particularly if a lot of fiddly detailed work is involved.

EDWARDIAN SILHOUETTES

Materials
Stiff grey-green cardboard, 13 × 10 ins for mount
Lime green cartridge (construction) paper, 10 × 7 ins for background
Thin black cartridge (construction) paper
Artificial flowers in assorted colours
Narrow white lace edging
Scraps of ribbon
1½ yds gilt braid
Fabric adhesive
Self-adhesive picture hanger

Method
Cut the cardboard and background paper to size. Stick the green paper on the mount leaving a 1½ in. border all round. Trace the outline of the silhouette (opposite) and cut out the shape very carefully. Place the paper pattern flat onto the black paper and draw round the outline with a white pencil. Cut out very carefully. Stick the figure and the parasol in the centre of the background and draw in the parasol handle and ferrule using a felt pen. Cut scraps of lace for the collar, cuffs, hem and parasol. Trim and stick into position. Stick ribbons and flowers in an attractive arrangement. Stick gilt braid all round the edge of the mount for a frame, mitring the corners to neaten them. Fix the picture hanger to the back.

APPLIQUÉ

Appliqué as defined by the dictionary means 'applied' or 'cut from one material or fabric and applied to the surface of another' – a rather unattractive way of describing a most attractive and decorative art. In appliqué, designs are cut out of fabric and applied to a contrasting background fabric in a variety of ways. This will depend on the use of the finished work – i.e. whether it is to be practical or decorative, and also on the material used.

If the finished piece of appliqué is to be a picture, then the areas of applied fabric do not have to be extremely well fastened, although it is usual to use decorative embroidery stitches to enhance the work. Where the finished work will have to withstand washing, ironing and constant wear, such as on children's clothes, aprons or other garments, the appliqués must be extremely securely fastened.

Methods of fastening include hand or machine embroidery, ordinary machine stitching, and neat handstitching. Nonfray materials such as leather, plastic and felt are particularly good to use for appliqué work as they can be stuck in position. Although appliqué is generally regarded as a form of decoration, if clothes have suffered a hedge tear, this can be mended and then covered by an appliqué shape. Besides being attractive, the appliqué gives added strength to the torn area.

As far as possible, the pieces of material to be applied to the background should be cut to follow the same grain as the background fabric. This helps to prevent the shapes puckering when the work is finished, but does not apply to leather, plastic and felt which are not woven and therefore do not have any grain. Because of this they can be cut in any direction and placed any way on the background fabric without fear of puckering.

Texture is important too. When making an appliqué picture for example, a rich variety of textures can be applied to the background fabric to create a sumptuous effect. Washable clothes, on the other hand, should have washable fabrics applied to them – and it is very important to see that they are colour-fast. Items such as cushions, curtains, bedcovers and garments which are likely to be dry-cleaned can have a variety of fabrics such as silk, satin, velvet, wool or lamé appliquéd on to the background. Appliqués of loosely woven fabrics such as hessian, nets, tweeds, open-weave furnishing fabrics and other materials which fray easily, should be used with care unless they are intended to give a shaggy texture to the work. The fraying can be allayed by applying a light coating of rubber solution or millinery glue, around the edges of the shape on the back only. This should be allowed to dry before the appliqué is placed on the background fabric. Alternatively, they can be ironed onto the iron-on type of self-adhesive bonded fabric, which is usually used as a fabric stiffener. The appliqués will then keep their shape and stay perfectly flat.

Methods of fastening

In all cases, the design of the appliqué motif must first be cut out from the contrasting fabric. Then it can be applied in a variety of ways.

By hand: If the appliqué shape is cut from non-fraying material, put it in position on the garment, and stitch it in place using a decorative embroidery stitch. Blanket stitch is most commonly used, but herringbone or feather stitch can also be worked and will give an attractive finish to the design. Use stranded embroidery thread, or if the appliqué is a heavy fabric itself, linen thread or tapestry wool will look very effective.

If you are using finer fabric for the shape you can overcome the fraying problem and give the shape more 'body' by cutting out the design in double thickness of fabric. Place the right sides of the shape together and seam round the edge leaving a small opening. Trim and clip round the edge, then turn the fabric through the opening so the right side is on the outside. Slip stitch the opening and then apply the shape to the background in the usual way.

'Blind' appliqué is done by hand, and is the technical way to describe appliqué where the raw edges of the shapes are turned under before the motif is sewn in place. The shapes in this type of appliqué should not be too complicated and it is usual to cut a straight or simple curved edge, otherwise the raw edges are difficult to turn under. To work 'blind' appliqué, make a paper shape or template of the design first, and pin and tack this to the right side of the fabric you are using for the finished design. Cut out the shape, allowing $\frac{1}{4}$–$\frac{1}{2}$ in. turnings round the paper template. Turn the edges of the shape under, in line with the edge of the paper, and tack them to the wrong side of the fabric. The shape then looks like a neat piece of paper with fabric turnings on the wrong side. Place the shape on the background, right side uppermost with the paper still in position. Stitch it down, using small slip stitches which should be invisible from the front of the work. Stitches used in 'blind' appliqué are not meant to enhance the design at all. Finally remove the paper and tacking threads from the front.

If you like you can give the appliqué more 'body' by using an interfacing material also, such as felt, iron-on fabric stiffener or paper. If you do so, tack or iron it onto the wrong side of the fabric shape and turn the raw edges over the interfacing. Tack the raw edges down, clipping any curves and apply the shape to the background material. As you do not remove the interfacing, the appliquéd design has a slightly raised effect.

By machine: A swing needle machine really come into its own here and can save endless time. Trace a design onto the fabric which is to be used for the appliqué. Baste this fabric into position with the design correctly placed over the garment and then, using the zig-zag stitch, machine stitch round the outside edge of the design on all sides. The stitches should not be too close together or the shapes will pucker. Neaten the thread ends and trim away all excess fabric right up to the edges of the zig-zag stitching, but tacking care not to clip into the stitching.

Iron-on appliqué: A selection of motifs and designs are commercially available and can be ironed straight onto the fabric to provide decoration. Alternatively, provided the appliqué fabric does not fray, a bonding material such as fuseable fleece can be used. Always carefully follow the manufacturer's instructions for use.

Appliqué aprons

The apron shapes on page 11 have been drawn out on squared paper with no allowance for turnings. Each square represents 1 in. Before you make any of the aprons, make a paper pattern using brown paper or newspaper for the aprons and the relevant motifs. The

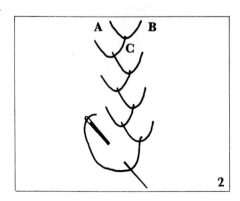

diagram on page 10 includes motifs which have not been used in our patterns. Use them to decorate other aprons of your own design or alternatively in picture making.

Stitches

As explained, various embroidery stitches, such as blanket stitch, herringbone stitch and feather stitch, can be used to appliqué motifs onto a background. Instructions for working herringbone stitch are given on page 18. How to work blanket stitch and feather stitch is explained below.

Blanket stitch: Working from left to right, take the needle through both thicknesses of fabric to the edge of the motif. With the thread underneath the point of the needle, pull the needle through and begin a new stitch in the same way (see diagram 1).

Feather stitch: Bring the needle out at A, insert it at B and bring it out again at C (see diagram 2). Keeping the thread under the needle, insert it again a little to the left on the same level and make a stitch to the centre, remembering to keep the thread under the needle. Repeat this procedure.

MAN'S GARDENING APRON

Materials

1 yd of 48-in. wide hessian or canvas
2 yds cotton binding 1 in. wide
Small felt squares for appliqué
Sewing thread in matching colours

Method

Using the pattern, cut apron shape and pocket. Allow $\frac{3}{4}$ in. turning all round plus a 2 in. hem at the bottom of the apron. Cut two apron strings $43\frac{1}{2}$ ins long (these are especially long so that they will tie at the front of the apron) and a neckband 25 ins long from the binding. Turn the edge of the apron over twice, inserting apron strings and neckband underneath the turned edge at the same time. Tack edge all around. Machine sew the turned edge with a double row of stitches. Cut out appliqué motifs in felt following the diagrams. Do not allow turnings as felt does not fray. Tack motifs in position on bib front and pocket. Machine sew round the edge of the appliqué. Tack the pocket in position turning raw edge under. Machine with double row of stitches. Turn up hem and stitch.

Note: The appliqué motifs on this apron could be made of strong cotton material. In which case the shapes must be cut out slightly larger and a narrow edge

Right: *top left: Man's Gardening Apron; top right: Little Girl's Apron; bottom left: Boy's Work Apron; bottom right: Kitchen Apron.*

turned under and tacked so that the material will not fray. When the shapes are placed in position on the apron the selvedge grain of the material should run downwards so that it will correspond with the background. This is important because the tension is then the same and the fabric is much less likely to pucker.

LITTLE GIRL'S APRON

Materials

$\frac{1}{2}$ yd felt
$\frac{1}{2}$ yd cotton material for lining
2 yds cotton binding 1 in. wide
$\frac{3}{4}$ yd coarse cotton lace
$\frac{3}{4}$ yd thin white cotton cord
Small felt squares for appliqué
'Invisible' thread
Fabric adhesive
(Apron fits 3–4 year old)

Method

Using the pattern, cut out apron and lining (both the same shape). Cut two apron strings 26$\frac{1}{2}$ ins long and neckband 18 ins long from the binding. Turn in edge of felt $\frac{1}{2}$ in. all round and tack. Insert apron tapes under the edge of the turning at the same time. Cut out felt appliqué shapes, following the diagrams. Arrange in position and tack them carefully onto the apron. Small pieces can be stuck lightly in position with fabric adhesive. Slipstitch round the shapes with 'invisible' thread. Cut and arrange white lace and cotton cord

in position. Tack and hand sew. Turn in $\frac{1}{2}$ in. edge around the lining. Lay the wrong sides of the apron and lining together. Tack and slipstitch the two together.

BOY'S WORK APRON

Materials

$\frac{1}{2}$ yd of 36-in. wide plastic coated fabric
3$\frac{1}{2}$ yds decorative cotton braid for edging and apron strings
$\frac{1}{4}$ yd contrasting plastic coated fabric for name appliqué
Sewing thread suitable for man-made fibres
Adhesive suitable for plastic coated fabric
(Apron fits 4–5 year old)

Method

Using the pattern cut out apron shape. Cut neckband 17 ins long and two apron strings 20 ins long from the braid. Turn $\frac{1}{2}$-in. edge onto right side of material all way round apron, and stick down lightly with a clear all-purpose adhesive. Tack the braid on top of this turning all round the edge of apron. At the same time, tack apron strings and neckband on to apron underneath the main braid outline. If a straight braid is used it must be eased round the armhole curvature with a series of small tucks. This problem will not arise if a bias binding is being used, but in this case a stronger, thicker, braid

will be required to make the neck and apron strings. Machine stitch the braid. Design and draw the lettering for the name on paper and trace on to the contrasting plastic coated fabric. Cut out and stick the letters in place on the apron using adhesive.
Alternatively, fix the letters in place with strips of adhesive tape. Machine stitch round the edges and then carefully remove the tape.

KITCHEN APRON

Materials

1 yd of 36-in. wide plastic coated fabric
$\frac{1}{2}$ yd of 2 contrasting plastic coated fabrics, one plain, one patterned
2 yds coloured tape 1 in. wide for strings
Sewing thread suitable for man-made fibres
Adhesive suitable for plastic coated fabric

Method

Using the pattern, cut out the apron shape and turn in $\frac{1}{2}$ in. all round. When turning this fabric it helps to stick in position with adhesive or adhesive tape before sewing as the fabric is too thick to tack properly and can show needle marks. Machine sew edges.
Cut out and turn in pocket edge all round. Sew top edge with double row of machine stitches. Place pocket in position on apron and machine in place with two rows of stitches. Cut out motifs

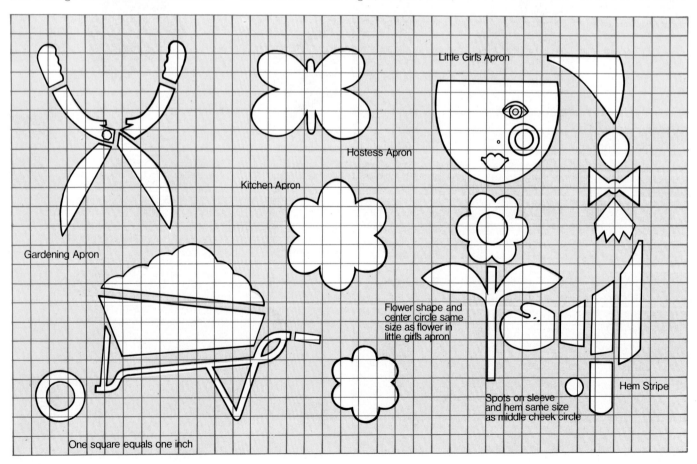

Little Girls Apron

Hostess Apron

Kitchen Apron

Gardening Apron

Flower shape and center circle same size as flower in little girls apron

Spots on sleeve and hem same size as middle cheek circle

Hem Stripe

One square equals one inch

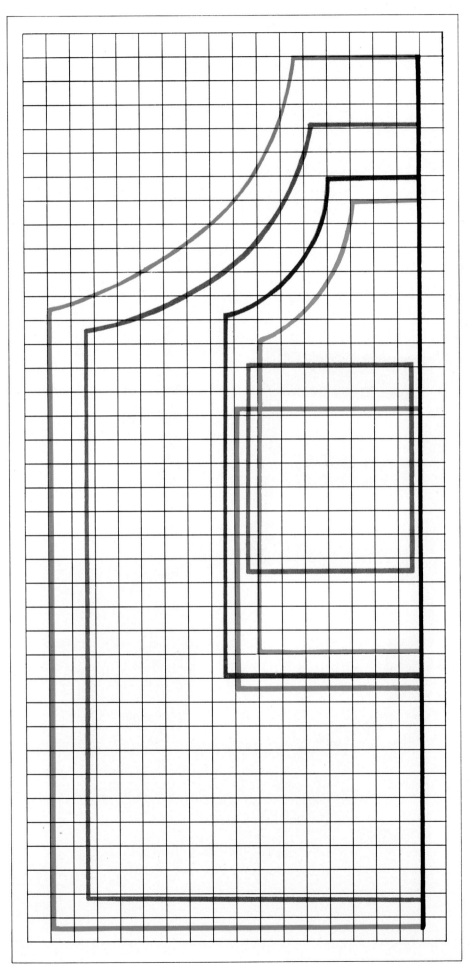

from contrasting coloured fabric following diagrams. Make sure surface of the plastic coated fabric is clean and dust free. Stick motifs in place with adhesive, or for extra strength, use an impact adhesive.

Place apron very flat with a weight on top of the motifs and if possible leave overnight. Check that edges of the shapes are glued down firmly. If necessary use a bit more glue on them.

Cut tapes into three 18-in. lengths and machine stitch to apron for neck tape and strings. Finish strings with neat hem.

ARAN KNITTING

Many countries have their own particular knitting patterns, for which they are known. A distinctive and very popular style has emanated from the island of Aran, and is now widely referred to as 'Aran knitting'. The patterns evolved through the knitting of thick warm sweaters, worn by the fishermen to combat the harsh weather conditions they encountered. These sweaters had different bands of pattern on the back, front and sleeves, and at one time it was said to be possible to tell from which village a man came, to which family he belonged and which son-in-the-line he was, just from his sweater!

The patterns of Aran knitting include honeycomb and diamond designs, zig-zag lines, raised 'bobbles', and the use of moss stitch and 'cable' stitch. Cable stitch produces a 'twisted' or 'woven' effect into the pattern and is done in stocking stitch using special cable needles in addition to ordinary knitting needles. At a certain point in the pattern a few stitches are slipped onto the cable needles and then knitted back into the row a few stitches further on, which gives the twisted effect.

All the stitches used in true Aran knitting were evocative of the country and fishermen's life. The cables, mentioned above, were the ropes and chains of the boats. The zig-zag lines were the twisting rocky paths that led down to the sea, and moss stitch or block stitches were used to indicate sand and shingle. The fishermen's nets are shown in the honeycomb and diamond patterns and the stout stone walls which protect the little homesteads from the fierce gales, and the rocks that present a perpetual danger to the fishermen, are represented by small knitted 'bobbles'.

The pattern given here uses the usual

knitting pattern abbreviations, an explanation of which will be found on page 5. In addition there are other abbreviations necessary to cover the different stitches found in Aran patterns. These are explained below.

c.n.	*Cable needle*
K.f.b. or p.f.b.	*K. or p. into front and back of next st.*
C3R	*(Cross 3 right) Sl. next st. on the c.n. and leave at back, k.2, then p.1 from c.n.*
C3L	*(Cross 3 left) Sl. next 2 sts. on the c.n. and leave at front, p.1 then k.2 from c.n.*
C4B	*(Cable 4 back) Sl. next 2 sts. on to c.n., leave at back, k.2, then k.2 from c.n.*
C4F	*(Cable 4 front) As C4B but leave 2 sts. on c.n. at front*
CP7	*(Claw Patt. 7) Sl. next 2 sts. on to c.n., leave at back, k.1, then k.2 from c.n., k. next st., then sl. foll. st. on to c.n., leave at front, k.2, then k.1 from c.n.*
Cross 5	*Sl. next 3 sts. on to c.n., leave at back, k.2, now pass the p. st. from other end of c.n. back on to left hand needle, bring c.n. to front, p.1 from left hand needle and lastly, k.2 from c.n.*
M.B.	*(Make Bobble) Into next st., work k.1, (w.fwd., k.1) twice, turn and p. these 5 sts., turn, k.5, turn p.5, turn. Now sl. 2nd, 3rd and 4th sts. over 1st and off needle, then k. tog. the rem. 2 sts. t.b.l. On next row, k. the st. over bobble tightly*

CUSHION AND LAMPSHADE

Materials

8 2-oz balls of Aran knitting wool for cushion cover and 6 balls for lampshade
1 pair each of Nos 7 (6) and 9 (4) knitting needles
1 cable needle
No. 8 (F/5) crochet hook
Lampshade frame, 9 ins deep × 44 ins circumference
2½ yds wool braid to match knitting wool
½ yd press stud tape
Tension: 5 sts. and 7 rows to 1 in. over st. st. on No 7 (6) needles
Measurements: Cushion cover – 17 ins square. Lampshade – as size of frame

Method

Cushion cover: with No. 9 (4) needles, cast on 101 sts and knit 1 row.
Next row: K.3, * p.1, (p.f.b., p.1) twice, k.f.b., (p.2, p.f.b.) 7 times, p.4, k.f.b., (p.1, p.f.b.) twice, p.1, * k.8, p.2, k.1, p.2, k.8, rep. from * to *, k.3. (127 sts.)
Change to No. 7 (6) needles and patt.
1st row: K.2, p.1, * k.7, p.2, k.32, p.2, k.7, * p.8, cross 5, p.8, rep. from * to *, p.1, k.2.

2nd row: K.3, * p.7, k.2, p.32, k.2, p.7, *, k.8, p.2, k.1, p.2, k.8, rep. from * to *, k.3.
3rd row: K.2, p.1, * CP7, p.2, (C4B, C4F) 4 times, p.2, CP7, * p.7, C3R, p.1, C3L, p.7, rep from * to *, p.1, k.2.
4th row: K.3, * p.7, k.2, p.32, k.2, p.7, * k.7, p.2, k.3, p.2, k.7, rep. from * to *, k.3.
5th row: K.2, p.1, * k.7, p.2, k.32, p.2, k.7, * p.6, C3R, p.3, C3L, p.6, rep. from * to * p.1, k.2.
6th row: K.3, * p.7, k.2, p.32, k.2, p.7, * k.6, p.2, k.5, p.2, k.6, rep. from * to * k.3.
7th row: K.2, p.1, * CP7, p.2, (C4F, C4B) 4 times, p.2, CP7 *, p.5, C3R, p.2, MB, p.2, C3L, p.5, rep. from * to *, p.1, k.2.
8th row: K.3, * p.7, k.2, p.32, k.2, p.7, * k.5, p.2, k.7, p.2, k.5, rep. from * to *, k.3. These 8 rows complete the patt. for double honeycomb and claw patt. panels. Cont. to keep these correct and at the same time, cont. with diamond

panel in the centre.

9th row: K.2, p.1, patt. 50, p.4, C3R, p.7, C3L, p.4, patt. 50, p.1, k.2.

10th row: K.3, patt. 50, k.4, p.2, k.9, p.2, k.4, patt. 50, k.3.

11th row: K.2, p.1, patt. 50, p.3, C3R, p.2, MB, p.3, MB, p.2, C3L, p.3, patt. 50, p.1, k.2.

12th row: K.3, patt. 50, k.3, p.2, k.11, p.2, k.3, patt. 50, k.3.

13th row: K.2, p.1, patt. 50, p.2, C3R, p.11, C3L, p.2, patt. 50, p.1, k.2.

14th row: K.3, patt. 50, k.2, p.2, k.13, p.2, k.2, patt. 50, k.3.

15th row: K.2, p.1, patt. 50, p.2, k.2, p.2, MB, p.7, MB, p.2, k.2, p.2, patt. 50, p.1, k.2.

16th row: As 14th.

17th row: K.2, p.1, patt. 50, p.2, C3L, p.11, C3R, p.2, patt. 50, p.1, k.2.

18th row: As 12th.

19th row: K.2, p.1, patt. 50, p.3, C3L, p.2, MB, p.3, MB, p.2, C3R, p.3, patt. 50, p.1, k.2.

20th row: As 10th.

21st row: K.2, p.1, patt. 50, p.4, C3L, p.7, C3R, p.4, patt. 50, p.1, k.2.

22nd row: As 8th.

23rd row: K.2, p.1, patt. 50, p.5, C3L, p.2, MB, p.2, C3R, p.5, patt. 50, p.1, k.2.

24th row: As 6th.

25th row: K.2, p.1, patt. 50, p.6, C3L, p.3, C3R, p.6, patt. 50, p.1, k.2.

26th row: As 4th.

27th row: K.2, p.1, patt. 50, p.7, C3L, p.1, C3R, p.7, patt. 50, p.1, k.2.

28th row: As 2nd. These 28 rows form patt. for diamond panel. Cont. until 8 complete patts. have been worked in this panel. Work 1st and 2nd rows again. Change to No. 9 (4) needles.

Next row: K.2, p.1, * k.1, (k.2 tog., k.1) twice, p.2 tog., (k.2, k.2 tog.) 7 times, k.4, p.2 tog., (k.1, k.2 tog.) twice, k.1, * p.8, k.2, p.1, k.2, p.8, rep. from * to * p.1, k.2. Cast off.

To make up: Fold work in half with wrong side out and join cast on and cast off edge. Press seam. Turn right side out. Along one side edge, work a row of double crochet through both thicknesses. Work a row of double crochet round the 2 sides of other edge. Sew press stud tape to opening. Insert cushion and fasten.

Lampshade: With No. 9 (4) needles, cast on 131 sts and work 3 rows g.st.

Next row: K.1, * k.8, p.2, k.1, p.2, k.8, (p.1, p.f.b.) twice, p.1, k.f.b., (p.2, p.f.b.,) 9 times, p.4, k.f.b., (p.1, p.f.b.) twice, p.1, rep. from * once, k.2. (161 sts). Change to No. 7 (6) needles and patt.

1st row: K.1, p.1, * k.7, p.2, k.40, p.2, k.7, p.8, cross 5, p.8, rep. from * once, k.1.

2nd row: K.1, * k.8, p.2, k.1, p.2, k.8, p.7, k.2, p.40, k.2, p.7, rep. from * once, k.2.

3rd row: K.1, p.1, * CP7, p.2, (C4B, C4F) 5 times, p.2, CP7, p.7, C3R, p.1, C3L, p.7, rep. from * once, k.1. Cont. in patt. as now set working 40 sts in

double honeycomb and other panels as on cushion. Work 58 rows in patt. Change to No. 9 (4) needles.

Next row: K.1, p.1, * k.1, (k.2 tog., k.1) twice, p.2 tog., (k.2, k.2 tog.) 9 times, k.4, p.2 tog., (k.1, k.2 tog.) twice, k.1, p.8, k.2, p.1, k.2, p.8, rep. from * once, k.1. Change to g.st., and work 3 rows. Cast off. Make another piece to match.

To make up: Place pieces together and join into a circle. Press seams. Fit over frame, placing seams over 2 of side supports. Catch the seams to supports. Fold g.st. edges over top and bottom of frame and catch down firmly, so that cover is stretched over frame slightly. Sew braid to top and bottom.

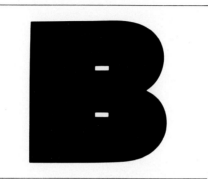

BATIK

The craft of Batik originated in Indonesia centuries ago and although the techniques involved may have become more mechanised over the years, they have basically changed very little. Batik is a process whereby patterns are drawn onto a piece of cloth with hot wax and the cloth is then dyed. The waxed areas repel the dye. The cloth may have to be waxed several times depending on the number of different colours that are wanted in the finished design.

Indonesian batik motifs all have special meanings, derived partly from primitive symbolism, but also influenced by Indian, Chinese and Arabic decorative art. Patterns may be definite in form and repeated at set intervals over the fabric, or free with no fixed repetition. The geometric patterns indicate the Indonesian influence, while the free forms are based on Hindu, and sometimes Chinese, designs.

Materials

White cloth: choose natural fibre fabrics such as cotton, linen and silk. If cloth feels stiff, wash in boiling water with soap and detergent to remove the finish (starch) and to give material a better affinity to the dye.

Wooden frame
Bowls
Jug
Spoons
Wax: 1 part beeswax/4 parts paraffin

wax
Solid pan or special wax pot
Heater
Iron
Newspaper
Rubber gloves
Salt
Soda
Drawing pins
Soft pencil
Tjanting, or Canting
Paint brush
Dye

Method

Pin the cloth tightly over the frame and draw on the design using a soft pencil. Heat the wax until a hazy blue smoke appears at which time it is ready to be applied to the part of the design you do not wish to 'take' the dye.

Wax may be applied with a paint brush or 'canting'. If you are using a canting for the first time, scribble with it on a remnant just to get the feel of it. Fill the 'pen' or 'bowl' with hot wax and then draw along the lines of the design letting the hot wax run out. It will probably run out very quickly and may form a 'blob'. Just continue along the line, making the 'blob' part of the design. Keep the canting at a steep angle so that the bowl part does not touch the cloth.

When waxing is completed, remove the cloth from the frame and crumple it beneath running cold water. The cloth must be wet before entering the dye to ensure even dyeing. Crumpling the cloth also cracks the wax slightly, giving the effect of streaks of colour appearing on a white or coloured background.

The cloth is then ready for the dye. Prepare the following two solutions separately:

1. The dye and warm-to-hot water (use a suitable dye for the fabric and follow the manufacturer's instructions.)

2. Salt, soda and warm-to-hot water (1 pint of water, 4 heaped tablespoons of salt and 1 heaped tablespoon of soda for each container of dye.)

Combine the solutions. Immerse the cloth in the dye bath and keep it moving by stirring with a spoon so that it dyes evenly. When dyeing is complete, rinse the cloth under cold water to remove all excess dye. You should continue rinsing until the water runs clear.

Hang cloth to dry away from heat, and preferably in a draught or near an open window. When completely dry, the cloth is ready for re-waxing. Pin back onto the frame and using a brush or canting, wax new areas of the cloth. Then re-dye it, using a different colour. Not only will the original areas be kept white but some of the recently dyed areas will retain the colour of the first dye. So a build-up of shape and colour has begun.

When all the dyeing processes have been completed, the cloth should be washed

(or boiled if this does not affect the dye) and ironed to remove all traces of wax.

LARGE SCARF

Materials
Fine silk or cotton, 27 × 27 ins
Dylon Dyes – Moon Blue, Radiant Pink, Nasturtium
Equipment listed under 'Materials', page 13

Method
Make the scarf following the pattern-marking, waxing and dyeing procedures already described. It will need three applications of wax and three dyeings as explained below:
First Waxing: Apply wax with a canting or fine paint brush as an all-over non-repetitive, floral design.
First Dyeing: Immerse in Moon Blue (a grey/blue). Hang up to dry.
Second Waxing: Re-wax new flowers and leaves, breaking into the Moon Blue ground.
Second Dyeing: Dye Radiant Pink. Hang up to dry.
Third Waxing: Re-wax more flowers over and between previous design.
Third Dyeing: Immerse in Nasturtium. Wash out wax, and iron dry.

BELT MAKING

Beltmaking is fun to do and the end results make marvellous gifts. You can use all kinds of materials. Ribbons and braids, for instance, mounted on belt stiffening, make colourful, gaily patterned belts; felt, trimmed with narrow braid and finished with eyelet fastenings, makes a charming peasant belt.
A sporty-looking link belt can be made from scraps of suede or leather and, of course, a belt worked in embroidery on canvas has a special cachet all of its own. Belts take comparatively little time to make and junk shops, you will find, are a treasure house for unusual buckles and clasps.

RIBBON AND BRAID BELTS

It is advisable to choose the buckle first and to have it with you when you are choosing the ribbon or braid. Not only

will you be able to make sure that you have chosen the best ribbon to enhance the buckle but you will also be able to check that the width of the ribbon fits the buckle bar.

Ribbons and braids are available up to quite wide widths. A 3 in. wide woven ribbon will make a superb belt used just as it is but consider the narrower kinds of braid as well. Sometimes, a ribbon or braid with a geometric design takes on a new and exciting look if two or more narrow strips are mounted side by side. If a single length of ribbon or braid is being used, buy a length to the waist measurements plus 6 ins. If narrower widths are being used mounted together to make a wide belt, multiply the waist-plus-6 ins measurement by the number of lengths you are planning to use.

Materials

Embroidered ribbons or braids
Belt stiffening or other stiff interlacing
Backing material such as taffeta or silk
Fabric adhesive
Suitable buckle
Strong all-purpose adhesive

Method

Cut a piece of belt stiffening or inter-facing to the exact width of the ribbon and to the waist measurement plus 6 ins. Cut one end of the stiffening into a point (see diagram 1) and then trim the two cut edges (A and B) back a further $\frac{1}{4}$ in. Trim the other short end of the stiffening (C) $\frac{1}{4}$ in.

Cut a piece of lining fabric to the width and length of the belt, (waist-plus- 6 ins), plus $1\frac{1}{4}$ ins on both measurements.

Place the stiffening down on the wrong side of the lining fabric and fold over the $\frac{5}{8}$ in. turnings all round. Mitre the corners neatly and fold the lining over the pointed end of the belt (see diagram 2). Glue the turnings down onto the stiffening using fabric adhesive but use very little or the adhesive may seep through and spoil the look of the inside of the belt. Place a weight on the pointed end and leave the belt to dry.

While the belt is drying, cut a point on the right hand end of the ribbon or braid. Clip $\frac{1}{4}$ in. into the point and turn under $\frac{1}{4}$ in. turnings. Turn the other short end of the ribbon under $\frac{1}{4}$ in. and press. To mount the ribbon, spread adhesive on the belt itself, not on the ribbon, taking the adhesive to within $\frac{1}{8}$ in. of the edges. This is so that any excess adhesive can spread a little without spoiling the ribbon or the lining. Use the minimum amount of adhesive and spread it as evenly as possible.

Place the ribbon down onto the glued surface of the stiffening and press it firmly into position with the flat of the hand. Leave the belt to dry. When quite dry, slip the buckle onto the square end – this is the left hand side of the belt so

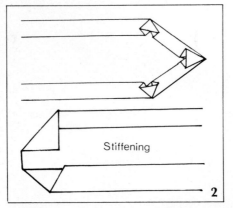

Stiffening

make sure that the buckle is the right way up if it is shaped – and fold the end of the belt under, over the buckle bar for about 2 ins. Glue the belt over the buckle bar using all-purpose adhesive and leave to dry under a weight. Secure with oversewing stitches.

FELT PEASANT BELT

Materials

Strip of $3\frac{1}{2}$ ins wide felt cut to the waist
   measurement plus 2 ins
Narrow braid or ribbon, twice the length
   of the belt plus 9 ins
6 eyelets
1 yd contrasting coloured silk cord

Right: *Embroidered belt.*

Below: *top: Belt made from decorative braid; below: Felt peasant belt.*

Method

Place the strip of felt on a flat surface and fold in the short ends 1 in. on the top side of the fabric. Glue these ends down. Cut two pieces of the trim, 3½ ins wide and mount these along the cut edges of the folded ends. Remember to use glue sparingly.

Cut the remaining trim into two equal lengths and glue along both long sides of the belt and over the short end strips. Turn ½ in. under at both ends to neaten. Make three equidistant marks on both edges of the belt fronts, ¼ in. in from the edge and insert eyelets.

Lace the belt together with the cord. (If eyelets cannot be obtained, finish off the holes with closely worked buttonhole stitch, using a brightly contrasting thread.)

EMBROIDERED BELT

Three embroidery stitches are used in the making of this belt. Chain stitch and stem stitch are used for decoration and herringbone stitch is used to attach the strip of interlining. How to work stem stitch is explained under Crewel Embroidery on page 34. Instructions for working chain stitch and herringbone stitch are given below.

Chain Stitch: Bring the needle out on the design line. Put it in again next to where the yarn was brought out. Pick up a small piece of the fabric along the design line, looping the yarn under the needle (see diagram 1). Pull the needle through, keeping the tension slack and repeat. The last stitch of a row is taken over the loop and back into the fabric to tie the loop in position.

Herringbone Stitch: Bring the needle through from the back. Lay the thread diagonally and with the needle horizontal pick up a small piece of fabric. Take the needle forward again and repeat along the row, (see diagram 2). The needle is in a horizontal position throughout the stitching.

Materials

Slub weave light brown linen, 30 × 9 ins
Non-woven interlining, 30 × 2 ins
Lining fabric, 30 × 6 ins
Belt buckle
5 skeins of Crewel Wool in varying shades of 'Autumn Yellow' colours

Method

(These instructions are for a belt to fit a

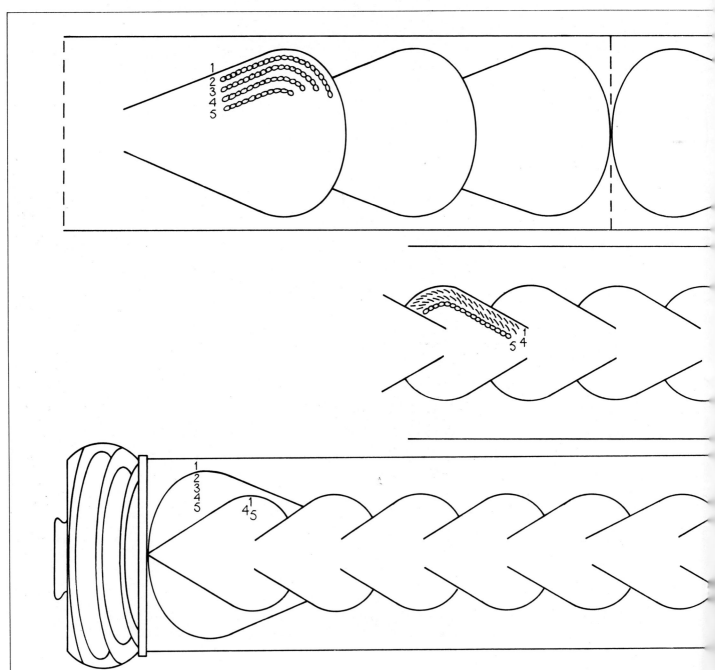

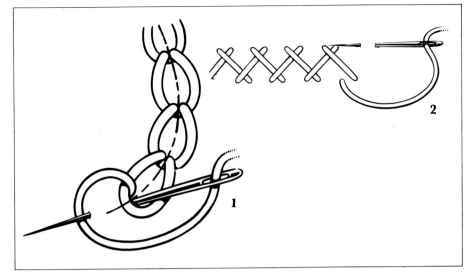

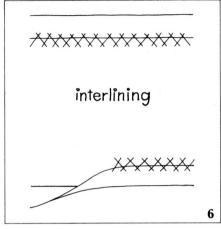

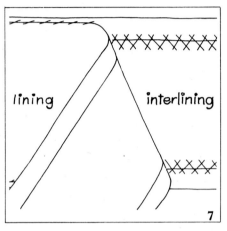

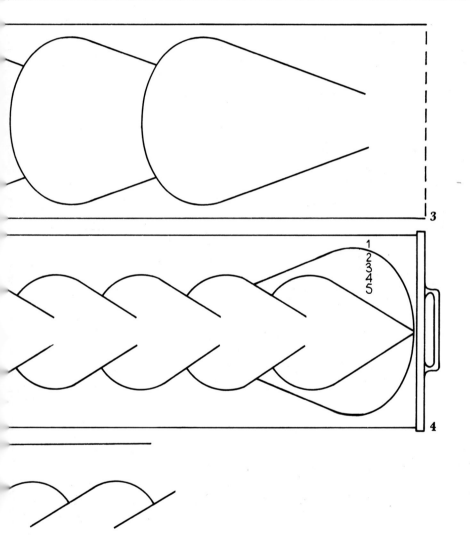

26 in. waist approximately.)
Cut a strip $30 \times 5\frac{1}{2}$ ins from the brown slub weave linen fabric. Oversew the edge to prevent the fabric fraying. With running stitch, mark the centre line down the length of the fabric. Transfer design to fabric, matching the centre lines, following diagrams 3, 4 and 5, (left) and the stitch and colour keys. All embroidery is worked with 3 strands of thread, except for the inner row of stem stitch which is worked with 2 strands. Press on the wrong side.

Tack the interlining to the centre on the wrong side. Trim seams to $\frac{1}{2}$ in. on the long sides. Herringbone the seam allowance to the interlining (see diagram 6). Turn in the seam allowance on the lining for the belt and trim excess fabric. Slip stitch to back of belt (see diagram 7). Adjust to waist size and thread the ends into the buckle links. Stitch firmly in position.

Stitch Key and Colour Key
∞∞ *Chain stitch,* ⧣⧣ *Stem stitch*
The colours are graded from the brightest through to the darkest. Thus No. 1, (shown in diagrams 3, 4 and 5,) indicates the use of the brightest yellow and No. 5, the darkest yellow. (See photograph of belt on page 17). Diagram 3 shows the centre back motif of the embroidered belt. Diagram 4 joins up with it on the right and Diagram 5 on the left, and show the right and left hand sides of the belt respectively.

BINCA EMBROIDERY

Binca is the name given to the canvas upon which this embroidery is worked. Made of cotton, it is unlike other embroidery canvas in that it is woven in blocks rather than individual threads. There are six of these blocks to 1 in. The nature of this weave really only makes it suitable for cross stitch embroidery – the more decorative but less uniform embroidery stitches would not only be more difficult to work evenly on the surface, but they would lose some of their attractive impact against this background.

Binca canvas is washable and is available in many different colours. It is attractive enough in itself to form part of the overall design, and does not need covering completely with embroidery. It is a particularly good canvas for children to use as the block weaving makes it easy to keep stitches regular and uniform.

The needlework bag, for which instructions are given below, is worked in cross stitch only, although a decorative form of hem stitch that looks effective is used to attach the handles.

BINCA NEEDLEWORK BAG

Materials

½ yd moss green Binca or Panama canvas, 42 ins wide, 6 squares to 1 in.
Stranded cotton thread as follows:
  2 skeins flame red
  2 skeins medium turquoise
  2 skeins white
Pair of wooden sewing bag handles, 13 ins wide
No. 21 tapestry needle

Method

Cut 2 pieces of Binca canvas 20 ins wide and 17 ins deep. (This is 2 ins bigger all round than the finished size of 16 × 13 ins, and allows for slight fraying of the edges when working.)

Beginning at the right hand corner, 2 ins away from each edge of the fabric, work the complete motif given in the diagram, in cross stitch. Work as for ordinary cross stitch (see page 39), but use six strands of cotton thread throughout and take it over one group of threads in the canvas in each direction. Work the motif twice more.

Work the smaller motif in the 2 spaces left between the larger motifs, embroidering the centre crosses in white thread instead of red.

To make up the bag, trim the Binca canvas to the finished size allowing an extra 1½ in. seam allowance and 1¼ in. hem allowance. With right sides together, machine stitch ½ in. away from

the edges, leaving the top open. Turn bag the right side out and then turn the 1½ ins hem allowance through the gap in the bag handles to the wrong side. Hem in place – keeping the threads of the fabric even, fasten the red stranded cotton ½ in. from the bottom of the hem on the right hand side at the back. Bring it through to the right side of the fabric at 'A' in diagram 1, and complete the hem stitch as shown.

Right: *Binca Needlework Bag*

Below: *Cross stitch chart for Binca Needlework Bag. The complete design is worked 3 times across the canvas, with the smaller motif worked twice more. The colour key is as follows:*
× *flame red* ● *medium turquoise* ○ *white*

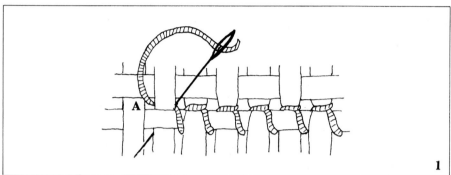

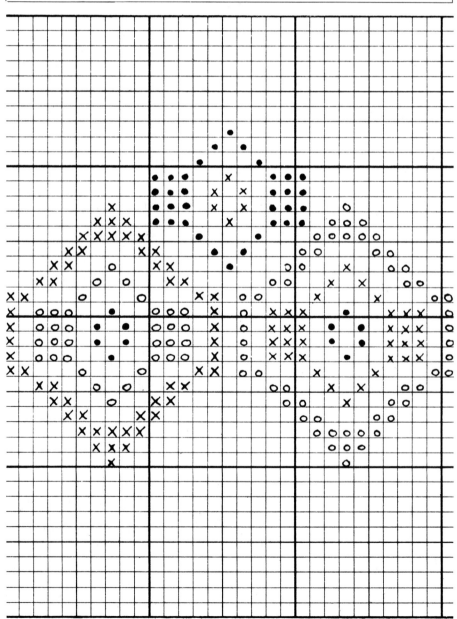

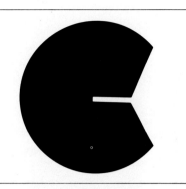

CANDLE MAKING

Candlemaking is a craft which everyone can enjoy. The basic materials for candlemaking are now widely available as the craft has gained so much popularity in recent years, but if trouble is encountered locally, most suppliers will send their goods by post. Moulds, wax, candle colours and wicks are all part of the candlemaker's basic equipment but if you want to make it an almost no-cost craft, old candles can be melted down and wax crayons used for colouring and decoration. Be sure to use good quality crayons – the colours are more subtle and the results more satisfactory.

We give instructions, (right), for making all sorts of candles using moulds and melted wax. However, expensive looking candles, with an 'oriental air' (see photograph on page 25), can be made using cheap, plain candles.

ORIENTAL CANDLES

Materials
Coloured crayons
Plain candles

Method
Peel some of the paper covering from a crayon. Warm the end of the crayon in a flame and dab it on the surface of the white candle. Cover the whole surface of the candle with random spots of contrasting colour. Then fuse the crayon spots to the candle by partially melting it in the flame of a candle (although this gives a slightly blackened effect) or a gas flame. Move the candle slowly in the flame and allow the wax to melt so the colours run into each other.

Variations using this simple basic method are endless. Try decorating a plain purple candle, for example, with heavy blobs of gold crayon or cover the whole surface of a pale pink candle with spots of deep pink and violet, running them into each other. Another idea would be to stripe the lower half of a blue candle with deep blue and green to create a subtle colour effect.

MELTED WAX CANDLES

Materials
A large supply of newspaper
Large and small metal containers for melting down wax
Sugar thermometer
Spoons
Sharp knives
Wooden sticks
Paraffin wax
Stearin
Candlewick
Candle colourings
Moulds of different kinds

Paraffin wax: Wax for candlemaking is supplied in solid blocks or in powdered form. Both are equally good but the powdered form is easier to use as the blocks have to be shaved down or broken up before melting.

Stearin: Stearin is a type of wax which allows wax dyes to dissolve readily and with complete colour suspension. It is not essential but it does produce a more opaque and intense colour and a more durable candle. It also acts as a mould release.

Candlewicks: Authentic candlewicking, available from candlemakers' supply shops, is bleached linen thread, woven and graded to burn a certain area of wax without smoking or excessive melting. It is essential to use the right grade of wick in a candle: a wick designated as 1 in. will successfully burn a candle 1 in. in diameter. It will also burn a 1 in. hole in a thicker candle which will result in the wick being drowned in a pool of wax!

If candlewick really is impossible to obtain, you can make candlewicking at home, but it is never quite so satisfactory. To make candlewick, use soft cotton string. Cut a length about 12 feet. Dissolve one tablespoon of salt and two tablespoons of borax in one cup of water. Put the string in the solution and let it soak for about 12 hours. Hang to dry out completely. When the string is dry, coat it by dipping in wax and use as directed.

Candle colours: Candle wax dyes are available in powder form and in discs. A small pinch of powder to a pint of liquid wax is usually enough to achieve a good colour. If the colour is too intense it can spoil the candle's glow.

Wax crayons can be used but experiment to make sure that you can achieve the effect you want.

Moulds: Craft shops sell an exciting selection of ready-made moulds for candlemaking but improvised moulds work very well and produce fascinating shapes. Many kinds of household containers can be used as long as they are leakproof and do not dissolve under the heat of melted wax. Some plastics will do this and so experiment with hot water first. Yoghurt and cream cartons, food cans, cardboard boxes and rubber balls are just a few of the things which can be used but remember that the candle has to be removed when set. The mould must therefore be able to be torn off the candle, or the neck must be large enough for the candle to slip out. Some cartons have a small mouth and a large base, and in this instance, the base can be cut off when the candle has set and the candle removed from this end. If cardboard moulds are used, oil the inside first so that the candle slips out more easily.

Method
Measure out the powdered or broken up wax. Measure out the stearin – 1 part stearin to 10 parts of wax. Melt the stearin gently in a saucepan and when dissolved, add the colouring agent. Melt the paraffin wax in a second saucepan and when this has melted, add the stearin colour mixture. Take care not to overheat wax and do not use water near it while it is hot or it will splutter and may cause burns.

The various temperatures for candlemaking are given with the specific instructions.

Moulded candles: Ready-made moulds, made of either latex or metal have no wick holes and these must be pierced with a needle. Dip the wick in wax to protect it then thread the wick through the hole and tie the other end to a wooden stick. Rest this across the top of the mould. Seal the hole and wick with mould seal or clay. (Plasticine will not do as it melts.) Support the mould by hanging it on a rack (see diagram 1, overleaf), which can be improvised by resting two long sticks across supports, such as books, flower pots etc. Heat the wax to 180°F and pour slowly into the mould. Tap the sides to release air bubbles. After a little while, a well will form round the wick as the cooling wax contracts. Prod the surface to break the skin and top up with wax, again heated to 180°F. Do this as often as the well forms. When the wax has completely hardened, peel back the surface of the mould with soapy hands. (The mould should be washed and dried carefully after use.) Trim the wick and polish the candle by rubbing it in your hands.

If the mould is a decorative one, colour can be added by mixing a little water paint with soap. Paint the candle, rubbing some into the crevices of the design and then rub most of the colour off just before it dries. Use water colour sparingly as it does not burn and may clog the wick.

If you are using an improvised mould, such as a soup can, pour the melted wax

Right: *A selection of candles that can be made at home. From left to right – round candle, zig-zag candle and star mould candles.*

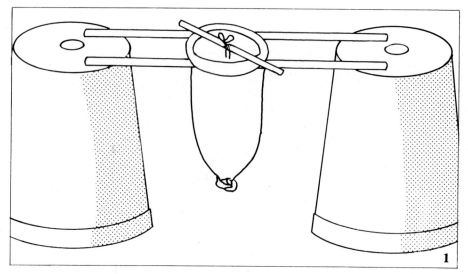

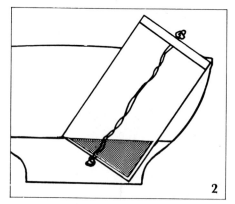

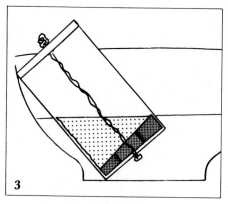

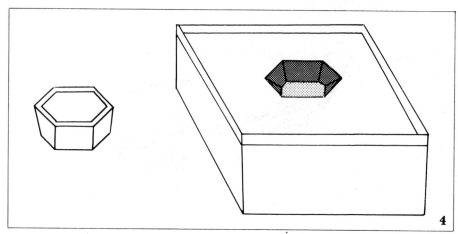

wax into round ice-cube moulds so that they are half full. When they have set, take them out of the moulds and fix them to the sides of a candle with wax glue. Then dip the candle into hot wax (230°F) to seal and gloss it.

Carved and Dipped candles: This type of candle involves a dipping technique, which is the oldest known method of making a candle. Fill a jug with wax heated to 180°F. The jug should be just deeper than the intended length of candle. Tie a short length of wick to a stick and dip it into the wax. Hold it in the air for about 30 seconds and the wax will harden. Dip again and again until the candle is thick enough. If a succession of different colours is used for dipping until each layer is about $\frac{1}{4}$ in thick, the completed candle can be carved back in some areas to reveal the different colours.

For a simpler surface decoration, try impressing a finished candle with various sharp objects such as nails or screwheads.

Twisted candles: Make these by flattening a dipped candle (see above) with a rolling pin while it is still soft. Hold the flattened strip in both hands and gently twist it. Then plunge the candle into cold water to harden it.

Layered candles: To make layered candles, have ready a large container of cold water. Pierce the can at the bottom and thread the wick through. Knot it underneath and then seal off with clay. Tie the other end to a stick and rest the stick across the can. Pour a little wax into the bottom of the can and stand it in the cold water, resting the can against the side of the container (see diagram 2). As each layer sets, pour in different coloured waxes, layer by layer until the can is filled (see diagram 3)

Sand candles: Fill a small box with damp sand. Dig a hole and push a small article such as a box, an ashtray, a cup or a bottle, into the sand (see diagram 4) to shape the hole as required. Remove the article. Heat the wax to 250°F and pour it carefully into the centre of the hole. Refill the hole as the level of the wax falls. Allow the candle to harden in a cold place for about 2 hours. Make a hole in the centre with a thin knitting needle and leave it standing in the candle. Leave to harden completely.

Next day, dig the candle out and brush away any loose sand. Remove the needle and insert a wick. Choose a wick which will leave some wax unburned – for instance, if the candle is 3 ins diameter, use a wick which will burn 2 in. The sand shell will remain after the candle has burned away and can be used again. Top up the hole round the wick with melted wax (220°F). You can now carve away areas of sand, but do not carve too deeply.

into the can (180°F), tie the wick to a stick and balance it across the top of the can. Leave to cool, topping up the well as before. Remove the hardened candle either by removing the bottom of the can and pushing the candle out or dip the can in hot water for a few moments. Make an unusual zig-zag candle, such as the one illustrated on page 23, using a glass mould. First cast 5 yellow, 5 red and 4 turquoise wax discs in an egg poacher. When they are set make a wick hole in the centre of each one. Thread the wick through so that the curved bases face alternately up and down. Drop the discs into the glass mould. Heat some very strongly dyed brown wax to 240°F,

pour it into the mould and shake the mould to release any trapped air. Cool the candle rapidly and release it from the mould. Carve out the zig-zags by hand and dip the candle into hot wax (230°F) to seal it and give it a gloss finish.

For a different effect, make a 'jewelled' candle. Break up pieces of different coloured wax and stick them round the insides of the can with a little melted wax. Pour the wax in little by little, so that it sets around the pieces without melting them. Alternatively dip pieces of coloured wax into melted wax and press these against the sides of a candle.

Another way to make a 'jewelled' candle, is to pour different colours of

to use a good quality, hard wearing type as it ensures a long life for the finished work.

There are two main basic types of canvas – single thread and double thread. The single thread canvases are usually easier to work with, but if the work is to include tramming stitches (see page 26), then double thread canvas, in which the warp and weft threads are arranged in pairs must be used.

Both types of canvas are graded according to mesh size. This is the degree by which the warp and weft threads are spaced out. A wide mesh will give fewer warp and weft threads to the inch; a fine mesh will give considerably more. In single canvas, the mesh size is referred to by the number of threads to the inch; in double canvas it is referred to by the number of holes to the inch. Mesh sizes range from 10 to about 32 threads or holes to the inch. There are also rug canvases available with only 3, 4 or 5 holes to the inch. These are excellent for working with thick wool to make quick bold designs.

The traditional threads to use for needlepoint are silk, wool and linen. It is possible, however, in a modern embroidery to use all kinds of novelty, 'special-effect' and other yarns. As long as the thread has hard-wearing qualities and is able to cover the canvas completely, it is suitable. It is important to remember that the thread should never be finer than the woven threads of the canvas being used, otherwise the canvas background will show through the stitches. Tapestry wool and crewel wool are both good-quality threads produced specifically for needlepoint, and rug wool, stranded and pearl embroidery threads can also be used successfully. Embroidery thread and crewel wool may be used in single or multiple strands as required to give adequate coverage to the canvas. Tapestry wool is only used in single strand. If a large quantity of yarn is required, to work a background for example, buy the full amount needed all at the same time, as any slight change in subsequent dye lots will probably be noticeable in the finished work. The wool that covers a background is known as 'grounding wool'.

Frames

Needlepoint embroidery stitches can be very roughly divided into straight stitches (i.e. those which follow the warp and weft lines of the canvas) and diagonal stitches (those which are worked across the canvas threads). If you intend to work only in straight stitches, then it is not necessary to mount your work on a frame although many people find a frame does give greater comfort and flexibility. Eliminating all the diagonal stitches from a design however, almost inevitably results in a loss of interest and variety. In

CANVASWORK

Needlepoint is probably the most traditional and still the most popular type of canvas work practised. It is mostly associated with beautiful cushion, chair and stool covers, usually in floral designs such as the one featured in our instructions and pictured on page 27, but more recently, needlepoint work has been extended to a range of modern, bold, often geometric designs, which make superb pictures and wall hangings.

The canvas is the background on which you work the needlepoint embroidery stitches. Although no canvas should be visible in the finished design, it is essential fact all the traditional stitches – tent, for example, cross and gobelin – are diagonal stitches. Unless the canvas is securely mounted in a frame, the strain of these stitches will gradually pull it out of shape, and distort the design. Use a rectangular slate frame for needlepoint, never a circular embroidery frame.

There are three basic types of frame to choose from, depending on the size and type of embroidery being worked: a leader frame which is a simple rectangular frame and has to be supported against a table or other suitable surface; a table frame which has its own adjustable support and can be placed on any table top; and a floor frame which is a free-standing, fully-adjustable frame similar in principle to an artist's easel.

Preparing the canvas

Cut the canvas 3 ins larger than the size of the finished piece of work. Note that canvas should always be mounted in the frame with selvedges at the sides.

Find the centre points of all sides of the canvas, before mounting, and mark them with lines of basting stitches worked in ordinary sewing thread and running right across the canvas. Turn ½ in. turnings to the wrong side at the top and bottom of the canvas and baste these to hold them in place. Bind these and the side edges of the canvas with 1 in. wide tape.

Framing up

The method of framing-up a piece of canvas is similar, whatever frame you use. Having prepared the canvas as explained, start at the centre point of one end and oversew this to the webbing attached to the rollers of the frame. Pull both canvas and webbing taut and use strong sewing cotton. Work outwards from the centre, first to one edge and then to the other, and fasten off the thread securely at both edges. Repeat the procedure, attaching the other end of the canvas to the other roller.

When both ends of the canvas are sewn to the webbing, put the side struts of the frame in place, slipping them through the slots at the ends of the rollers, and fixing them with the split pins. Fix one roller first, then stretch the canvas so it is taut before putting in the split pins at the other end. If the canvas is larger than the frame, wind it round the rollers before fixing the pins in position. The canvas working surface should be as tight as a drum, and this can be further ensured by sewing a strip of webbing down each side of the canvas, through which tapes or strong twine are threaded and tied securely round the side struts at regular intervals. These pieces of webbing must not be longer than the exposed working surface, or else the edges of the canvas would tighten up while the centre remained slack.

Therefore, when it becomes necessary to wind on the canvas, the webbing must be removed from the sides and re-attached to the new working area.

Besides keeping the canvas in good shape, the other reason for using a frame is to leave both hands of the worker free to work the stitches. One hand should be kept above the canvas and the other beneath it, so that the needle can be passed easily up and down through the correct holes in the canvas. It is essential, therefore, that the frame is placed in a comfortable working position.

Stitches

Tramming: This is an important tapestry embroidery technique which helps to give a rich appearance to the finished work. It also increases the hardwearing qualities of the design. Tramming is a type of ground work: long stitches are laid across the canvas, before beginning the embroidery stitches. When the background is completely covered with tramming, embroidery is worked over it, giving a double covering of thread to

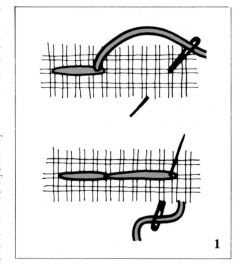

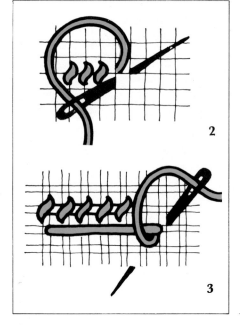

Right: *Traditional Needlepoint Cushion.*

the canvas. Tramming should be worked in the same colour and type of thread as the finished design.

To work split trammed stitch, which is the tramming stitch most suitable for covering large areas of canvas fairly quickly, bring the needle through from back to front of the canvas at the point where a pair of vertical threads cross a pair of horizontal threads. Work from left to right. Carry the thread along horizontally for a distance not greater than 5 ins then pass the needle through the canvas at a similar crossing of threads (see diagram 1).

Bring the needle back through one vertical thread of the canvas to the left on the same line, through the stitch just made, thus forming a split stitch. Continue in this way to cover entire area where tramming is required.

Tent stitch: This stitch is sometimes known as petit point. It is worked without tramming and may be worked on single or double thread canvas. If worked on the latter the threads of the canvas should be opened up and the stitches worked over separate, single threads.

To work tent stitch bring the needle out on the left-hand side of the area to be covered, and on the top part of the first stitch. Work from left to right. Pass needle diagonally down over one horizontal thread of the canvas, and one vertical thread to the left. Bring needle back out of the canvas two vertical threads to the right and one horizontal thread up (see diagram 2). Continue in this way.

When the first row is completed, work the second row from right to left. This time, in order to maintain the same slant of stitch, pass the needle up and over the crossed thread and then under two vertical threads.

Trammed tent stitch: This stitch is sometimes known as gros point. It is simply tent stitch worked over a tramming base. Tramming and tent stitch can be worked concurrently in the following way: work a trammed stitch from left to right, then pull the needle through and insert again up and over the crossed threads. Pull the needle through on the lower line two double threads to the left in readiness for the next stitch. Work tent stitch over the trammed stitch from right to left (see diagram 3). When the stitch is covered bring the needle out between a crossing of canvas threads on the line below, and repeat the sequence working trammed stitch first from left to right, then tent stitch over it from right to left.

TRADITIONAL CUSHION

Materials

½ yd double thread canvas, 19 ins wide, 10 holes to 1 in.

Colour key

⊡ Carnation	⊞ Violet (dark)	◧ Forest Green (dark)	⊞ Amber Gold (medium)	◉ Terra Cotta (dark)
⊃ Magenta	⊙ Lilac (light)	◥ Moss Green	◪ Amber Gold (dark)	⊠ Sage Green (light)
⊠ Cyclamen (light)	⊟ Lilac (dark)	⫼ Muscat Green (light)	◐ Tangerine	⊤ Sage Green (dark)
■ Cyclamen (dark)	⊻ Jade (light)	⊠ Muscat Green (dark)	⊟ Terra Cotta (pale)	☐ Petrol Blue
⋀ Violet (light)	⊙ Jade (dark)	∣ Canary Yellow	◲ Terra Cotta (light)	◺ Pink (pale)
	⊡ Forest Green (light)	↗ Amber Gold (light)	⊞ Terra Cotta (medium)	⊠ Pink (dark)

28

½ yd velvet or similar mediumweight fabric, 36 ins wide to match petrol blue background thread
No. 19 (18) tapestry needle
Cushion pad, approx. 16 in. square
Tapestry wool as follows:
  21 skeins Petrol Blue
  1 skein each of:
  Carnation
  Magenta
  Cyclamen (light and dark)
  Violet (light and dark)
  Lilac (light and dark)
  Jade Green (light and dark)
  Forest Green (light and dark)
  Moss Green (light and dark)
  Muscat Green (light and dark)
  Canary Yellow
  Amber Gold (light, medium and dark)
  Tangerine
  Terra Cotta (pale, light, medium and dark)
  Sage Green (light and dark)
  Pink (light and dark)
(N.B. The finished embroidery measures 16 ins square. The large diagram shows the complete centre floral motif. Each background square on the diagram represents the double threads of the canvas.)

Method

Prepare the canvas and place it in a frame.

Begin the embroidery in the centre and work following the diagram and the guide to thread colours. The black arrows on the diagram mark the centre and should coincide with your basting stitches.

The main flower heads on the diagram have been outlined in order to make the design more clear. Work the embroidery throughout in trammed tent stitch.

Continue background on all sides of the central flower motif until work measures 16 ins. (Note – as you have only ½ yd of canvas, 19 ins wide, you will not in this instance be able to have the usual minimum of 3 ins unworked canvas around the design.)

Trim canvas to within 1 in. of embroidery on side edges. Cut a square measuring 18 ins from backing fabric. Place embroidery and backing fabric together, right sides facing, and stitch close to the embroidery round three sides. Trim seams and turn cover to right side. Insert cushion pad, turn in seam allowance on remaining open edge, and slipstitch neatly together.

COLLAGE

Collage is essentially an enjoyable and creative handicraft. It involves few rules, and those that there are can easily be broken if they don't fit in with your design.

Collage is simply the application of different shapes and decorations onto a background in order to build up a picture or design. The choice of materials and how they are assembled is always up to the person making the collage, which means there is a great opportunity for individual expression and for making something truly personal. Get into the habit of collecting possible 'collage' components so you always have a store of things to choose from. Such things as oddments of fabric (all types, but 'rich' fabrics such as velvet, hessian, brocades, felt, furnishing fabrics, lace etc. are particularly good); small pieces of trimmings, ribbons and braids; sequins, beads, buttons, artificial and dried flowers, bits of fur; feathers; scraps of coloured wools, raffia and string; shells, unusual shapes of pasta

and pebbles; seeds; foliage; scraps of kitchen foil and coloured paper – are all useful in collage making.

The application of design components to a background is probably best done with an adhesive of some sort. Make sure you use a suitable adhesive for the material involved – for example a special fabric adhesive for heavier fabrics and trimmings (used sparingly so it does not mark the fabric), a wallpaper paste for paper and lightweight fabrics and a clear all-purpose adhesive for harder objects. Double-sided tape is invaluable in collage too as it is so quick and clean to use. If you are only using fabric to make a collage, you could sew the pieces in place with small invisible stitches. Choose your background materials to suit the design and set off the subject. Textured fabrics such as coarse weaves or thick hessians are very attractive. Keep the basic design of a collage simple and not too small as this gives more scope for development and last minute detail. If you find inspiration lacking, start off by looking at greetings cards, posters, magazines, books – or other pictures! The basic equipment you need apart from the materials themselves and the adhesives already mentioned, is simple and minimal – a pencil, ruler, paper (including tracing paper), large scissors, small pointed embroidery scissors, pins, a craft knife and possibly a T-square, compass and pair of tweezers.

THE BRIDAL COUPLE

A helpful way to begin the craft of collage is by working a collage design onto an existing picture or illustration. The original subject and background can be used and will help you in the choice of suitable materials. The illustrations on this page show how a greeting card can be turned into a collage. It is unlikely of course that your choice of card will be the same as the one shown here. However, in order to simplify the instructions we have explained how to do this specific collage. The methods and principles involved will apply to any card you use, or indeed, any collage picture or design which you may choose to make.

Materials

Greeting card or illustration
Scraps of:
  black felt, blue flock-spotted organza, fine cotton lace, scalloped lace trimming, narrow white satin ribbon, green guipure lace daisies, stranded embroidery thread, green raffia, green tissue paper, green taffeta ribbon, small pink lace and velvet flowers.
Tiny pearl buttons and silver sequins
Fabric adhesives and paste
Pair of tweezers
Tracing paper

Method

Study the subject on the card or illustration, then start with the main or basic garments of the figures, or with the central object. In this case, this is the man's suit and the girl's dress and veil. Make careful tracing paper patterns of these outlines. Cut out man's suit from black felt, by pinning the tracing pattern to the felt and cutting round the outline. (Felt does not fray so it is an ideal material to use. If you are using a fabric which frays badly, back it with iron-on fabric stiffener before cutting). Cut out the girl's dress from flock-spotted organza, and the veil, in three pieces, from fine cotton lace. Put in position on the card, but don't stick down yet. (When you reach a similar stage in your design, place the main pieces on the illustration and then plan the small details before proceeding with glueing.)

Cut man's collar and cuffs from scraps of lace and glue in place. Then stick down the suit and the girl's dress. Cut out scalloped lace trimming for the skirt and bodice, green guipure lace daisies and individual pink flowers.

Stick in position. Make a small bow from narrow white satin ribbon. Glue in place and top with a daisy and flower. Use adhesive sparingly all the time.

Next apply the hair. Use six-stranded embroidery thread. Cut each piece to length and soak in paste before sticking it in position. Begin at the outer edge so you can add top and front pieces to overlap any stray ends. Use tweezers and pointed scissors to guide the strands into position. Glue the veil, daisies and flowers in position on top.

Build up the bouquet by glueing on crumpled green tissue paper and covering it with leaves cut from taffeta ribbon, and the pink flowers. Accentuate flower stalks with narrow strips of green raffia. As a final touch, glue tiny pearl beads round the flowers in the girl's hair and bouquet and a silver sequin as an earring.

NURSERY COLLAGE

This collage is especially interesting because it incorporates several different crafts. The background is coloured with special dye paint, which is also used for the flowers and the pattern on Mrs Bear's dress. The tree is effectively made from scraps of fabric that has been patterned with tie-and-dye work. Shoe dye is used to paint details on the suede bears and the tree trunks. The hessian house is appliquéd with embroidery thread to give the impression of bricks. Other details are made from scrap fabrics, glued into position. The shapes on the collage have been kept simple.

Materials

$\frac{3}{4}$ yd white cotton furnishing satin
4 sachets Dylon Paintex
4 sachets Dylon Cold Dye fix
Tins of Dylon Cold Dye in blue, green, navy, red and orange
1 bottle Miss Dylon (or other) suede dye in black smoke colour
Scraps of yellow velvet, hessian, felt, suede, rick-rack, lace
12 circular red buttons
1 square button or bead for door handle
Fabric adhesive
Piece of thick cardboard 26 × 22 ins
Black and red embroidery thread and needle

Method

Using the graph pattern of the complete picture (below right), draw up the design to the correct size and transfer the outline to white fabric (see pages 42 and 43). The scale of the graph pattern of the whole picture is 1 square = 1 in. Also make tracing paper patterns of the house, the bears and their clothes. Make up blue and green Cold Dye with Paintex, following manufacturer's instructions. Using an ordinary paint brush, paint in sky and grass onto the fabric, leaving white spaces for flowers, and window. Now make a darker green colour by mixing the made-up blue and green dye paint together. Use this to paint in leaves for the flowers. Leave the fabric to dry, then wash and rinse to remove surplus paint. Press when dry.

Make two 'tie-and-dye' trees from scraps of green fabric and brown suede (see Tie-Dye, page 114). The dappled effect on the leaves is obtained by crumpling yellow velvet into a ball and then binding it tightly before dyeing it with the navy blue Cold Dye. Remove bindings. Crumple into a ball again and bind tightly. Dye a second time, using green Cold Dye. Untie bindings, dry velvet, then press lightly.

Make tracing patterns of the tree shapes (see diagram 1). The scale of diagram 1 is 4 squares = 1 in. Cut out 3 of each of the 'leaves' shape from the dyed velvet, and 2 tree trunks from scraps of brown suede. Stick into position. Paint on the shadows with suede dye following the manufacturer's instructions. Sew each of the red buttons on to a green velvet shape. Stick shapes in place so they overlap.

Cut out the 3 bears from scraps of brown suede using your tracing pattern. Stick them on to the collage. Paint in their faces, paws and toes with the suede dye. Cut out Mr Bear and Baby Bear's clothes from scraps of felt and stick on to collage.

Prepare the red and orange Cold Dye and mix with Paintex, following the manufacturer's instructions. Cut out Mrs Bear's dress from yellow velvet. Paint on the pattern free hand, using the red and orange dyes. Use the red also for painting in flowers on the background fabric. Stick Mrs Bear's dress in place when the Paintex is dry.

Cut out the house from hessian, leaving a space for the door and window. Use orange felt for the roof and sun. Sew scraps of lace to background cloth where the window will go. Baste the house on top and stitch into place with blanket stitch to look like bricks. Sew long black threads across the window to look like glazing bars. Cut out door from green felt. Sew on button for the handle and stick door in place. Stick on orange felt roof, painting in tiles with suede dye. Add greenery by the door, made from

1

scraps of tie-and-dye velvet.

Stick on sun rays, using scraps of yellow rick rack. Cut out a circular sun from orange felt and stick this in the centre of the rays. Stretch the wall hanging over the cardboard base so that it looks smooth, then stick it firmly to the back of the cardboard. Attach strong cord to the back to hang up the collage.

CREWEL EMBROIDERY

'Crewel' is the term given to the highly spun, two-ply wool which is used to work this kind of embroidery. It is however, a deceptively simple term for a richly varied style of embroidery that flourished particularly between the mid-seventeenth and mid-eighteenth centuries. At that time crewel embroidery was most dramatically used on bed hangings and the traditional designs of exotic flowers and animals, the Tree of Life theme, unicorns, griffins, fruits, flowing leaves and twining branches were curved and twisted into elaborate and colourful designs. Later the art was carried across to New England, USA, where it assumed a lighter feel and a greater mellowness of colour.

As with so many of these delightful 'older' crafts, crewel embroidery is enjoying a current revival, and can be used to execute the traditional patterns or to create modern exciting designs.

Any fabric which is firm to handle will support crewel wool embroidery. Linen twill is the traditional fabric for crewel work. It is thick and hard wearing and usually a creamy colour. It looks at its best with a bold pattern worked on it, which will complement the weight of the fabric. Plain weave linen, which is available in a wide range of colours looks good with a small scale design with fine stitchery that stands out clearly on the smooth surface. Slub weave linen or cotton takes textured stitches to advantage, although for a rich effect, it is necessary to use two or more strands of yarn. Fine details tend to be lost on this surface. It can be seen from this that the design worked and the stitches to be used will affect the choice of fabric to some extent, so make sure you have some idea of the finished design before choosing the fabric.

When you buy fabric, take a colour choice of crewel wool along with you and compare both the colour, and the weight of the wool, with the colour and weight of the fabric. Bear in mind the object you are going to make as well. It will be hard to make up a small object, such as a spectacle case, if you use a thick fabric on which to work the embroidery. If you are making a practical object, a tray cloth for example, choose an easy-care fabric.

Stitches

The embroidery stitches used in crewel embroidery are important as they make up the texture of the finished work. The relation of one stitch to another creates a play of light across the surface of the design, and each stitch has its own particular quality. One or more strands of wool can be used when working – the more strands used, the larger the stitches will be. Work with a short length of yarn, about 18 ins, to avoid the wool becoming knotted or rubbed. Practise the different stitches comparing the effect when worked with differing numbers of strands. Each person's embroidery will have a different tension and you may need to experiment to achieve the visual effect you want. Remember embroidery is at its best when it makes a clear definite pattern on the fabric. The final result will be disappointing if the overall effect is thin, or too thick and clumsy.

The stitches explained individually below are those used in our lampshade pattern, but of course there are many other embroidery stitches used in crewel embroidery. They can be roughly divided

Right: *Crewel Embroidery Lampshade*

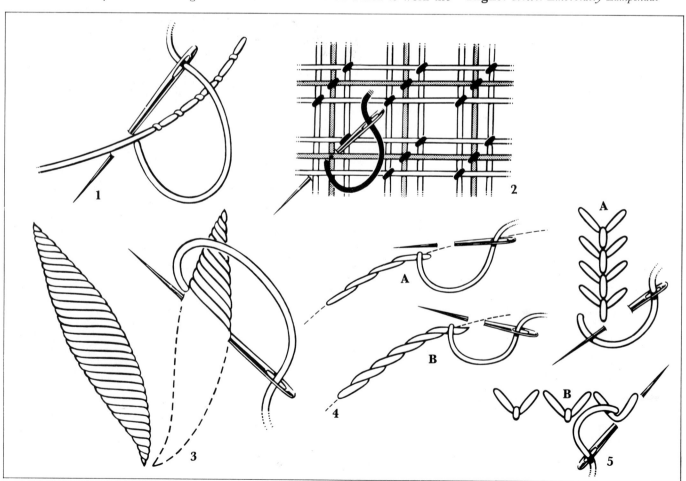

into three groups – flat, looped and knotted.

Couching: This is a line or filling stitch. Work it in a frame. Take the end of a long piece of yarn through to the back of the fabric. This may be a very thick yarn or a fine cord. Thread a double loop into a heavy needle and use this as a lever to pull the heavy yarn through. Thread a second needle with a finer matching or contrasting yarn. Lay the thick yarn along the design line and tie it down at intervals with a short stitch taken at right angles to the design (see diagram 1, previous page).

Battlement couching: Three different colours are used in this stitch. Lay three lots of even threads horizontally and vertically. Tie down the points of intersection of each lot with small slanting stitches (see diagram 2).

Satin stitch: This is a very easy stitch to work, but it needs practice to do it really well. Straight stitches are repeated side by side. Bring the needle up from the back of the fabric. Take it down so that the thread lies vertically across the stitch area. Bring the needle up again beside the point at which the yarn first came out. Repeat along the row. Work it in a frame in two movements. Bring the needle up from the back, lay the thread and hold it in position with the left forefinger. Return the needle to the back and draw the yarn through so that it lies lightly on the surface of the fabric (see diagram 3).

Use this method for all flat stitches which need to lie smoothly side by side.

Stem stitch: Also easy to work, this stitch is very versatile. It can act as a single, fine line, a raised, or a broad line.

Bring the needle up from the back and put it in again a little in advance of the previous stitch (see diagram 4).

For a fine line, bring the needle up just above the previous stitch (A).

For a broader line, bring it out to one side (B). For a raised line, work it over a laid thread.

Make the stitches smaller when following a tight curve, lengthen them on a straight line.

Fly stitch: Work this as grouped, but individual stitches. Repeat one below another (A) or side by side as line stitches (B). Bring the needle out at the left of a centre line. Put it in at the opposite side and bring it out again on the centre line to form a 'Y' shape. Loop the yarn under the needle, return it at centre line and repeat (see diagram 5).

LAMPSHADE

Materials

2 yds × 18 ins wide cream surface-embroidery linen

Lampshade frames including support bracket (see diagram 1, below right). (Diameter of frame should be 20 ins)

White glossy paint (see 'Method')

2 yds iron-on adhesive parchment

$\frac{3}{8}$ in. lampshade tape

$\frac{1}{2}$ in. bias binding trimming or braid

Fabric adhesive

Strong sewing thread and silk thread to match linen

Crewel wool as follows:
    5 30-yd skeins of Drab Fawn (dark)
    2 30-yd skeins each of:
    Drab Fawn, Flesh Tint, Mid-Blue,
    Bright China Blue, Purple, Rose Pink,
    Bright Rose Pink (light and dark)
    1 30-yd skein each of:
    Dull Marine Blue, Heraldic Gold
Crewel Embroidery needle, medium-size
No. 9 sharps needle
Clothes pegs

Method

Enlarge the design shown below and transfer it to the embroidery linen (see pages 42 and 43). Repeat the pattern as necessary to fit right round the shade. Following this design pattern, the detailed diagrams of small areas marked A and B (below, right), and the keys for colour and stitches, work the embroidery along the surface of the linen. Press on the wrong side of the fabric.

If the lampshade frame is made of unpainted metal, give the frame two coats of white, glossy paint, to prevent rusting.

Bind top and bottom rings with tape. Cut parchment to exact size of lampshade frames so that ends of parchment touch but do not overlap. Place parchment on a flat, smooth surface, shiny side up. Lay embroidered material right side up on the parchment making sure that there is a $\frac{1}{2}$ in. margin of material all round. Press firmly with hot iron. Allow to cool before handling.

Sew side seams together so that both ends of the parchment meet. Make a 'drum' (see diagram 2, below right) by fitting the material onto the frames, holding the frames and material in position with clothes pegs. Oversew the lampshade to the top and bottom rings of the frame using a No. 9 sharps needle and matching silk thread. Work the stitches on the outside edge of the ring from right to left.

Trim away surplus material from top and bottom of the lampshade, cutting close to the stitches.

Measure the circumference of the top of the shade and cut two strips of bias binding. Glue the bias binding round the upper and lower rings, covering the stitches, and turning the binding over to the inside of the frame too.

Stitch key

※	*Battlement Couching*
#	*Couching over 1 laid strand*
##	*Couching over 2 strands*
⋎	*Fly Stitch*
⧺	*Stem Stitch*
≡	*Satin Stitch*

Colour key

1 *Mid-Blue*
2 *Drab Fawn (dark)*
3 *Bright China Blue*
4 *Dull Marine Blue*
5 *Drab Fawn (light)*
6 *Flesh Tint*
7 *Rose Pink*
8 *Purple*
9 *Bright Rose Pink*
10 *Heraldic Gold*
11 *Bright Rose Pink*

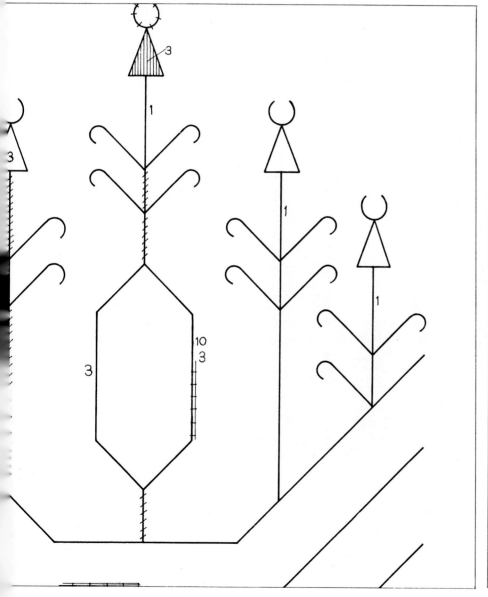

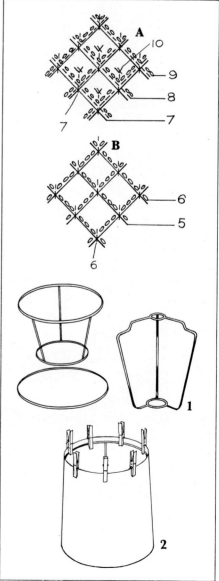

35

needed in all crochet work. Hooks are available in steel for working with fine cotton yarns and in aluminium or plastic for coarser or synthetic yarns.

HAT, SCARF AND BAG

Materials
Hat: 1 1-oz balls Double Knitting wool (knitting worsted) in rust, camel, black and white
Scarf: 2 1-oz balls Double Knitting wool (knitting worsted) in rust, camel, black and white
Bag: 2 1-oz balls Double Knitting wool (knitting worsted) in rust, and black and 1 1-oz balls in camel and white
No. 8 (F/5) and No. 9 (E/4) crochet hooks
1¾ yds of 1½ ins wide petersham or stiff ribbon
½ yd lining for bag
Measurements: The hat is average hat size, the scarf is 6 ins wide and 68 ins long, excluding the fringes. The bag is 10½ ins in diameter.
Abbreviations: For crochet abbreviations, see page 5. In addition, R = rust, C = camel, W = white, B = black.

Method
Hat: * * With No. 8 (F/5) hook and R, make 5 ch. Join with s.s. to form a ring.
1st round: 2 ch., 11 tr. (d.c.) into ring: 12 sts. Join with s.s. in 2nd of 2 ch.
2nd round: In R, 2 ch., * 2 tr. (d.c.) in next st.; rep. from * ending with 1 tr. (d.c.) in base of 2 ch.; 24 sts. Join with s.s. Join in B.
3rd round: In B, 2 ch., * 2 hlf tr. (h.d.c.) in next st., 1 hlf tr. (h.d.c.) in next st.; rep. from * ending with 2 hlf tr. in last st.: 36 sts. Join with s.s. Join in W.
4th round: In W, 2 ch., 1 hlf tr. (h.d.c.) in each st. all round. Join with s.s. Join in C.
5th round: In C, 2 ch., * 2 tr. (d.c.) in next st., 1 tr. (d.c.) in each of next 2 sts; rep. from * ending with 1 tr. (d.c.) in last stitch.: 48 sts. Join with s.s.
6th round: In C, 2 ch., * 2 tr. (d.c.) in next st., 1 tr. (d.c.) in each of next 3 sts; rep. from * ending with 1 tr. (d.c.) in each of last 2 sts: 60 sts. Join with s.s.
Note: Carry yarns loosely up back of work.
7th round: In W, 2 ch., * 2 hlf tr. (h.d.c.) in next st., 1 hlf tr. (h.d.c.) in each of next 4 sts; rep. from * ending with 1 hlf tr. (h.d.c.) in each of last 3 sts: 72 sts. Join with s.s.
8th round: In B, as 4th * *.
9th round: In R, 2 ch., * 1 tr. (d.c.) in each st. all round. Join with s.s.
10th round: In R, 2 ch., * 2 tr. (d.c.) in next st., 1 tr. (d.c.) in each of next 5 sts; rep. from * ending with 1 tr. (d.c.) in each of last 4 sts: 84 sts. Join with s.s.
11th round: As 8th.

Right: *Child's Cross Stitch Apron.*

CROCHET

Traditionally associated with fine lacy patterns, used to make table mats and dressing table runners, modern designs, colours and yarns have greatly widened the scope of crochet as a craft. Attractive clothes, toys and imaginative personal and household articles can all be made in crochet and a mass of different effects can be quickly and easily worked once the basic technique has been mastered. The term crochet is derived from the French word 'crochet' meaning hook – which is the basic piece of equipment

12th round : As 4th.

13th round : In C, 2 ch., 2 tr. (d.c.) in next st., 1 tr. (d.c.) in each of next 6 sts; rep. from * ending with 1 tr. (d.c.) in each of last 5 sts: 96 sts. Join with s.s.

14th round : In C, as 9th.

15th round : As 4th.

16th round : As 8th.

17th and 18th rounds : As 9th.

19th round : As 8th.

20th round : As 4th.

21st round : As 14th.

Change to No. 9 (E/4) hook.

22nd round : As 14th.

23rd round : As 4th.

24th round : As 8th, but turning work and working with wrong side facing all round. Join with s.s. Fasten off.

Scarf : With No. 8 (F/5) hook and B, make 301 ch.

Foundation row : In B, 1 hlf tr. (h.d.c.) in 3rd ch. from hook, 1 hlf tr. (h.d.c.) in each ch. to end: 300 sts.

Join in W and pattern as follows:

1st row : In W, 2 ch., miss 1st st., 1 hlf tr. (h.d.c.) in each st., ending with 1 hlf tr. (h.d.c.) in 2nd of 2 ch. Join in C.

2nd and 3rd rows : In C, 2 ch., miss 1st st., 1 tr. (d.c.) in each st., ending with 1 tr. (d.c.) in 2nd of 2 ch.

4th row : As 1st.

5th row : In B, as 1st. Join in R.

6th and 7th rows : In R, as 2nd and 3rd.

8th row : As 5th. These 8 rows form pattern.

Note : Carry yarns loosely up sides of work.

Repeat rows 1–8 inclusive, then 1st row again. Fasten off.

Bag : Work as for hat from * * to * *.

9th round : In R, 2 ch., * 2 tr. (d.c.) in next st., 1 tr. (d.c.) in each of next 5 sts; rep. from * ending with 1 tr. (d.c.) in each of last 4 sts: 84 sts. Join with s.s.

10th round : In R, 2 ch., * 2 tr. (d.c.) in next st., 1 tr. (d.c.) in each of next 6 sts; rep. from * ending with 1 tr. (d.c.) in each of last 5 sts: 96 sts. Join with s.s.

11th round : In B, 2 ch., * 2 hlf tr. (h.d.c.) in next st., 1 hlf tr. (h.d.c.) in each of next 7 sts; rep. from * ending with 1 hlf tr. (h.d.c.) in each of last 6 sts: 108 sts. Join with s.s.

12th round : In W, 2 ch., 1 hlf tr. (h.d.c.) in each st. all round.

13th round : In C, 2 ch., * 2 tr. (d.c.) in next st., 1 tr. (d.c.) in each of next 8 sts; rep. from * ending with 1 tr. (d.c.) in each of last 7 sts: 120 sts. Join with s.s.

14th round : In C, 2 ch., * 2 tr. (d.c.) in next st., 1 tr. (d.c.) in each of next 9 sts; rep from * ending with 1 tr. (d.c.) in each of last 8 sts. Join with s.s.: 132 sts.

15th round : In W, 2 ch., * 2 hlf tr. (h.d.c.) in next st., 1 hlf tr. (h.d.c.) in each of next 10 sts; rep. from * ending with 1 hlf tr. (h.d.c.) in each of last 9 sts: 144 sts. Join with s.s.

16th round : In B, as 12th. Fasten off. Make another circle the same.

Handle : With B, make 261 ch.

Foundation row : 1 hlf tr. (h.d.c.) in 3rd ch. from hook, 1 hlf tr. (h.d.c.) in each ch. to end: 260 sts. Break B. Join in R.

Next row : In R, 2 ch., miss 1st st., 1 tr. (d.c.) in each st. ending with 1 tr. (d.c.) in 2nd of 2 ch. Rep. last row twice more. Break R. Rejoin B.

Next row : 2 ch., miss 1st st., 1 hlf tr. (h.d.c.) in each st. ending with 1 hlf tr. (h.d.c.) in 2nd of 2 ch. Fasten off.

To make up : Using a warm iron and damp cloth, press each piece of crochet lightly on wrong side. Darn in short ends of yarn on wrong side.

Scarf : Cut remaining yarn into 12 in. lengths to make a fringe at either end of scarf. Using 6 strands together each time, double yarn and knot into short ends of scarf, alternating colours as shown in the illustration. Trim fringes.

Bag : Cut 2 circles of cardboard 10 ins in diameter, then cut 2 circles of lining, each 11 ins in diameter. Place a cardboard circle in centre of each lining circle and glue ½ in. turnings of lining on to card, clipping at intervals to make a neat fold. Sew lining and card circles to each crochet circle, wrong sides together,

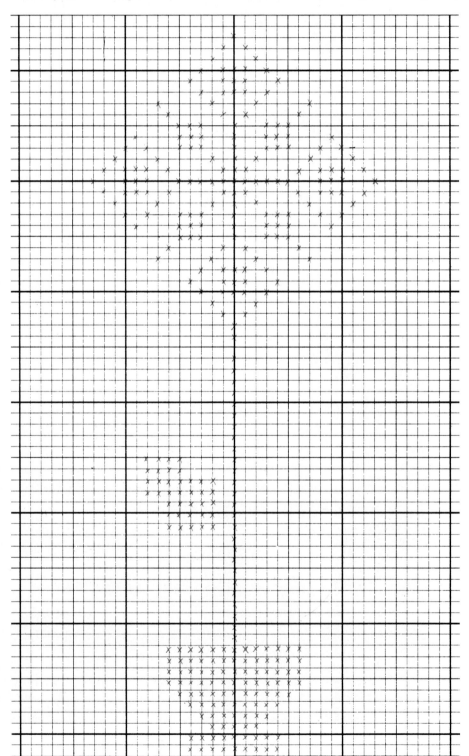

38

catching edge of lining circles ¼ in. away from outer edge of crochet circles. Join short ends of handle together. Cut petersham 1 in. longer than handle. Join short ends together ½ in. away from end. Press join open. Pin petersham in centre of handle, wrong sides together and sew in position all round.

Pin join on handle at point on circle where work was fastened off. Count 48 sts on circle and handle from this point in each direction and mark with pins. Using No. 9 (E/4) hook and B and with right side of handle facing, crochet bag and handle together in d.c. between the 2 marked points. Fasten off and work other side to correspond.

CROSS STITCH

Cross stitch is an extremely attractive and effective stitch to use in decorative work. It is very easy to do, but looks at its best, if it is really regular and even. Cross stitch is worked from left to right and is easiest to do on a fabric with an even weave or a checked pattern. Bring the needle through at A (see diagram 1), and work a row of sloping stitches all over the same number of threads. Return to the starting point and make another

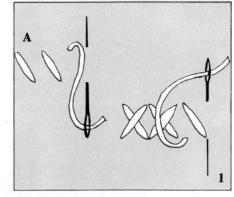

row of stitches over the top of the first row, as shown in the diagram.

CHILD'S CROSS STITCH APRON

Materials
½ yd 36-ins wide pink gingham (with ¼-in. squares)
Matching sewing thread
2 skeins of royal blue, six-stranded embroidery thread
1 card of dark blue bias binding
Tracing paper and paper 15 × 17 ins

Method
Enlarge the diagram below by dividing the piece of 15× 17 ins paper into 1 in. squares and copying the pattern (see pages 42 and 43). Trace the pattern onto tracing paper. Trace the pockets separately.

Cut out the apron shape and two pockets, two waist ties 18× 3 ins and one neck tie 16× 3 ins from the pink gingham.

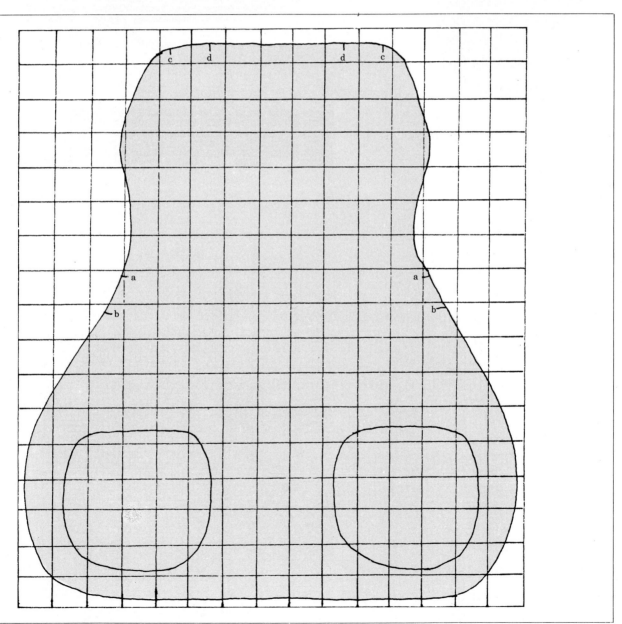

Mark the vertical centre line of the apron with a line of basting stitches and, using this as a placement line for the flower stalk, start to embroider the cross stitch design shown on the chart on page 38, 1 in. away from the bottom edge of the apron. Use three strands of embroidery cotton throughout.

To make up, bind all the way round the outside edge of the apron with the blue binding. Then bind the pockets in the same way and machine stitch them in position. Fold the waist and neck ties in half lengthwise, wrong sides together and turn under ½ in. on the long side and each of the ends; topstitch with the machine, ⅛ in. away from the edge. Sew the waist and neck ties in place as indicated in the diagram on page 39.

also looks most effective worked as a decorative embroidery stitch. It is at its best done on an evenweave, open-mesh fabric such as embroidery linen, net, canvas or huckaback, and if worked entirely alone, i.e. not in conjunction with other embroidery stitches, it may be used to create a pattern motif itself, or to fill in a background so that the motif is formed by the fabric left unstitched. It is quick and easy to do, but, in common with other simple stitches, needs to be very evenly worked if it is to be shown off to greatest advantage.

Traditional designs using darning decoratively comprise fairly simple patterns worked in and out of the meshes of the fabric, with bright colours of thread. It is a particularly effective way of decorating table, bathroom and bedroom linen.

Stitches

Darning stitch: Used in design work, this is similar to a long basting stitch worked to give a decorative effect.

Work from right to left, picking up only one thread of the fabric with each stitch (see diagram 1). The fabric threads which are picked up should form a pattern, as well as the darning stitches themselves, so it is important to space stitches evenly. Use an open-mesh weave which allows you to count the fabric threads.

Double darning stitch: This is a variation of the basic darning stitch which is useful for building up a flat surface

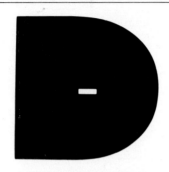

DECORATIVE DARNING

The simple utilitarian darning stitch need not only be used for mending – it

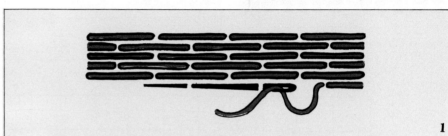

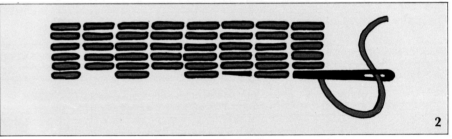

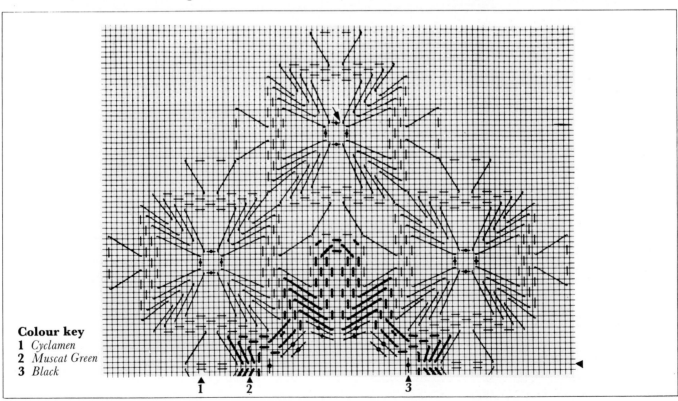

Colour key
1 *Cyclamen*
2 *Muscat Green*
3 *Black*

filling. Work one row of darning stitches from right to left, spacing the stitches evenly so the length of the stitch and the length of the fabric picked up are equal. Then work a second row of stitches from left to right, filling in the gaps left on the first row. On this second row insert the needle into the fabric and bring it back out at the same holes as on the first row (see diagram 2).

Darning on net: This technique can be used to make patterned net curtains, fine bedspreads, or even a bride's veil.
The important rule to bear in mind with this form of darning is that the thread used should be thick enough to fill the mesh of the net exactly – neither too thin, so it drags the net, or too thick so it distorts it. With a coarse-mesh net, wool is the best yarn to use; with finer net fabric, stranded cotton is suitable, as then the appropriate number of strands can be used to fill the mesh of the net exactly.

Darning on huckaback: As huckaback has a pronounced and regular weave, it makes an ideal background for darning embroidery. Attractive and unusual

towels can be quickly and inexpensively made in this way.
Stranded cotton again is the best yarn to use. Work darning stitches, as previously described, but, just taking the stitches under the loops of the fabric. Nearly all the stitching will then be on the surface of your work.

SWEDISH DARNING TABLECLOTH

Materials
Stranded thread as follows:
  11 skeins cyclamen
  3 skeins muscat green
  1 skein black
2¼ yds of 59-in. wide beige evenweave embroidery linen – 21 threads to 1 in.
No. 21 (20) tapestry needle

Method
Mark the centre of the fabric both ways with lines of basting stitches.
The diagram (left) gives a little more than half the complete motif.
Each of the background lines on the

diagram represent the threads of the fabric. The right hand arrow should coincide with your crosswise basting stitches. The design is worked throughout in darning stitch; the diagram shows the arrangement and length of individual stitches on the threads of the fabric.
Using 6 strands of cotton throughout, begin the embroidery with one short side of fabric facing you, start the stitching at the small black arrow 28 threads down and 127 threads to the right of crossed basting stitches. Work the section of design shown in the diagram, following the key to thread colours given. Work in reverse from the blank arrow to complete the motif. Repeat the motif three more times immediately below as shown, leaving 22 threads between each motif, and then complete lower right-hand quarter.
Work lower left-hand quarter to correspond. Turn fabric and work the other half of the design in a similar way. Press embroidery on wrong side. Turn in 1 in. hems on all edges, mitre the corners and slipstitch neatly in place.

41

DESIGN

Designs and patterns for finished articles are frequently given in reduced sizes. These need to be enlarged and transferred – or if they are the correct size, transferred only – to the material. This is actually very simple.

Enlarging a pattern
Patterns are usually given on a squared, graph-type diagram, with a scale indicating the size each square of the graph represents. Estimate from this the size of the overall area of the finished pattern and mark out onto a large sheet of tracing or tissue paper. Divide this space into the same number of vertical and horizontal lines as shown on the small design, and rule them up using a ballpoint pen.

Number the squares on the small diagram and also on your ruled paper. Then transfer the design from each small square to the corresponding large square (see diagram 1). If there are a lot of curved lines on the pattern itself, rule in any vertical or horizontal ones first, using a sharp pencil. Then put a 'dot' mark on the lines of your enlarged design to correspond exactly with the places where the line of the pattern falls on the lines of the graph diagram. Join up the dots when you have marked them all, following the curves of the pattern on the graph.

To save ruling up the actual lines of the graph, you can purchase squared dressmaker's paper which is sold in large sheets and marked in $\frac{1}{2}$ in. and 1 in. squares.

If the pattern you have copied is a design motif for embroidery, there are a number of ways of transferring it to the fabric where it is to be worked (see right). Use the method that is most suitable for the fabric and the design.

If you have copied component parts, or all of a pattern that is to be cut out in fabric and made into a garment or article, make sure you also mark on all the figures, words and marks from the graph diagram. Cut out the pattern pieces from the squared or ruled paper and either use these as actual pattern pieces to be pinned to the fabric for cutting out, or if you want to use the pattern again, make a tracing duplicate of the component pieces and use those. The simplest method of all to enlarge a design is to take it to a photostat concern that handles blueprints and other photostats. This will cost a small fee, but saves a lot of time and ensures a perfect enlargement. It is particularly useful if designs are given 'free-standing' – i.e. not in the form of a graph diagram.

Transferring the design to the fabric
Before you begin to transfer an embroidery motif to the fabric, check that the cut edges of the fabric are even by pulling a thread and cutting to the straight weave.

Positioning the design correctly onto the fabric is an important part of preparation. It is not difficult and takes little time, but is well worth the small amount of trouble as it makes all the difference to the finished appearance of the design. Where the embroidery will fill the centre of the fabric, measure and run a basting thread for the vertical and horizontal centres.

2

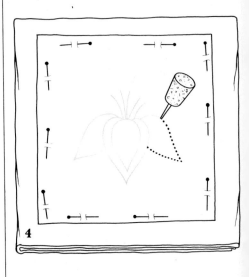

4

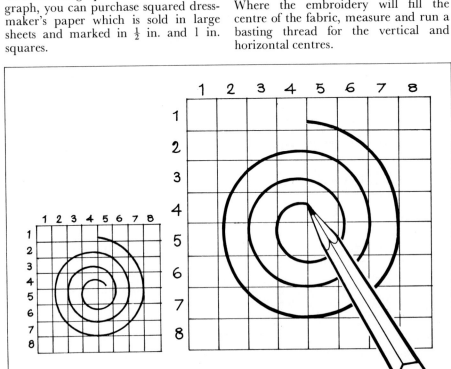

1

6

3

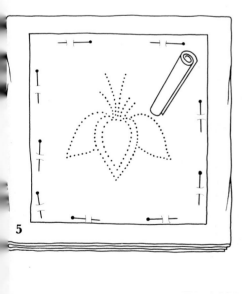

5

Either stitch marking lines by basting along the straight weave of the fabric, or mark them with pins.

Use any of the following methods when transferring the design, but be careful with the transfer pencil method, in which the design is pressed on with a hot iron. Pins would mark the fabric, so use the basting method in this case.

There are four methods of transferring the design to the fabric.

Transfer Pencil Method: All you need besides the design drawn onto tracing paper, is a transfer pencil and an iron. Sharpen the pencil to as fine a point as possible. Draw very lightly over the design lines on the wrong side of the tracing paper. Short strokes are better than a continuous line (see diagram 2). On a large design, sharpen the pencil several times so that the lines remain fine. The design can now be used in the same way as a commercial transfer. Pin it face down onto the fabric and press with a hot iron. *It is important to keep the drawing fine as the line spreads with the heat from the iron.*

If you want to reverse your design, draw with the pencil on the right side of the tracing paper. The design will iron-on in reverse so make sure you have the transfer line drawn in the correct position for the embroidery.

Tissue Paper Method: Besides the design enlarged and drawn up onto tissue paper, you will need a fine sewing needle and cottons in similar colours to the embroidery yarns you will be using to work the actual design. Work on a large flat surface and pin the tissue paper design in position on the fabric. Outline the design with running stitches, taking a smaller stitch on the surface than under the fabric (see diagram 3). You will find that being able to see where colour changes occur, makes it quicker and easier to work the final embroidery.

When you have stitched all round the outlines in running stitches, remove the pins. Hold the stitches flat with the forefinger of your left hand and gently tear away the paper from the sewn lines with your right hand. This way, the design will keep its shape.

This method is excellent for marking simple, bold shapes and the only satisfactory way for transferring designs to a slub fabric.

Prick and Pounce Method: This is a traditional method used by many craftsmen for transferring a design to a working surface. It is not suitable for a slub or textured weave as the design will not show up sufficiently. Besides the design you wish to transfer drawn onto tracing paper, you will need a fabric pad, a small roll of felt, some powdered tailor's chalk and charcoal and a fine paint brush and water colour paint. In addition, push the eye end of a fine needle into a cork – this makes a good 'pricker'.

Lay the embroidery design onto a pad, such as a folded blanket. Then, using the cork and needle pricker, prick holes at regular intervals along the design lines (see diagram 4). Space the holes evenly and not too closely or the paper will tear.

When you have pricked all round the design outline, lay the tracing in position on the fabric. Sprinkle with powdered white tailor's chalk if you are working on a dark fabric. If you are working on a light fabric, mix the tailor's chalk with a little crushed charcoal before sprinkling it. With the small roll of felt, rub the powder through the holes (see diagram 5). Carefully remove the tracing paper, and paint over the lines, using water and a fine brush. When this is dry, gently shake the surface powder from the fabric.

Carbon Paper Method: This method is successful on smooth, plain-weave fabrics. You will need dressmaker's carbon paper – use white for a dark fabric and yellow for a light fabric – and a tracing wheel.

Lay the fabric on a smooth surface and cover the design area with carbon paper. Put the traced design on top taking extra care in positioning it to make sure it is straight in relation to the grain of the fabric. (The carbon paper will be concealing the grain).

Pin the 3 layers together and then press firmly round the outline of the design with the tracing wheel (see diagram 6).

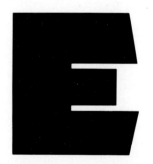

EMBROIDERY

We have discussed various types of embroidery previously in this book; for example, crewel embroidery on page 32, cross stitch embroidery on page 39 and decorative darning on page 40.

All these involved the use of stitches exclusively, but exquisite embroidery patterns can also be created by incorporating other materials such as beads, sequins, unusual braids or scraps of textured fabrics into the design. The overall effect can be further enhanced by mixing various types and thicknesses of thread, perhaps introducing some rich metallic or gold and silver ones.

The design is especially important in this kind of embroidery, particularly in terms of the relationship the different materials and threads have with one another. If you are creating your own design, you should always sketch it out first, experimenting with different shadings as you go along. Note the textures of the objects you want to use and which way they lie, the different shapes and effects made by the colours and the soft or angular quality of the lines which hold all the objects together.

Stitches

The only conventional embroidery stitch used in our evening bag pattern, is satin stitch (described on page 34). In addition overcasting or oversewing is used to apply some of the shapes. This is a stitch, probably used less often in embroidery than in sewing and dressmaking when it is useful to bind raw edges to prevent them fraying, or to hold two edges together. Work left to right, as shown in the diagram below, with small diagonal stitches taken through both thicknesses of fabric.

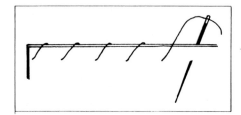

EVENING BAG

Materials

½ yd of 36-ins wide evenweave yellow furnishing (upholstery) fabric
A piece of pale lemon silk Duppion fabric 15 × 9 ins
A piece of cotton wadding, 6 × 11 ins
Scraps of yellow and white felt
Small pieces of gold and lemon kid
¼ yd gold and iridescent braid, 1½ in. wide
1 reel (ball) of gold thread
1 ball of pale lemon chenille wool (yarn)
1 reel (ball) of pale lemon thread
1 ball of lemon perle cotton, thickness No. 8
1 skein of white stranded cotton
4 rectangular lemon plastic shapes with holes in them (if you cannot find any, use acetate as a substitute)
22 ¼ in. brass studs
18 barrel-shaped gold beads
3 square gold painted wooden beads
12 large and 25 small round gold-painted wooden beads
26 bright yellow beads
100 small white chalk beads
80 small gold beads
10 semi-circular white beads and 8 medium and small-sized white beads
3 gold tambour beads
Kapok for padding
Embroidery needles

Method

Make the pattern for the design, by dividing a piece of paper, 11 × 6 ins into 1 in. squares and transferring the design pattern from diagram 1, enlarging it accordingly. Make the pattern for the bag by dividing a piece of paper, 19 × 19 ins into 1 in. squares and enlarging and transferring the shape from diagram 2, overleaf (see page 42 and 43).

Trace the enlarged design and transfer it to the right side of the Duppion fabric by putting carbon paper face down on the fabric and drawing over the lines

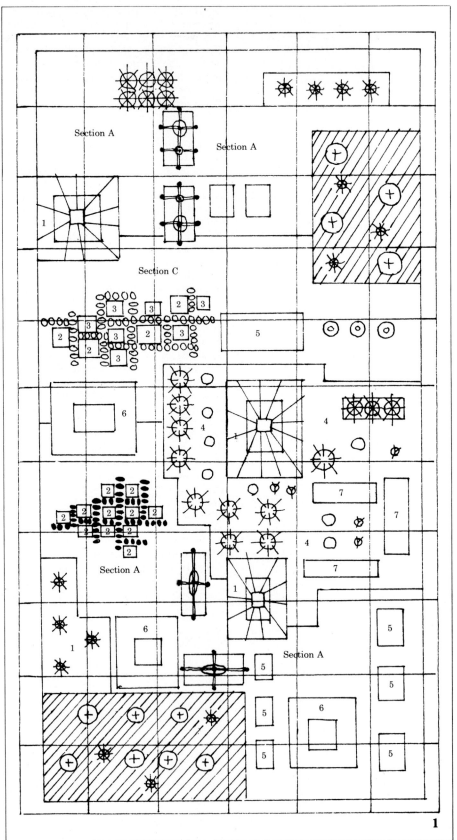

1

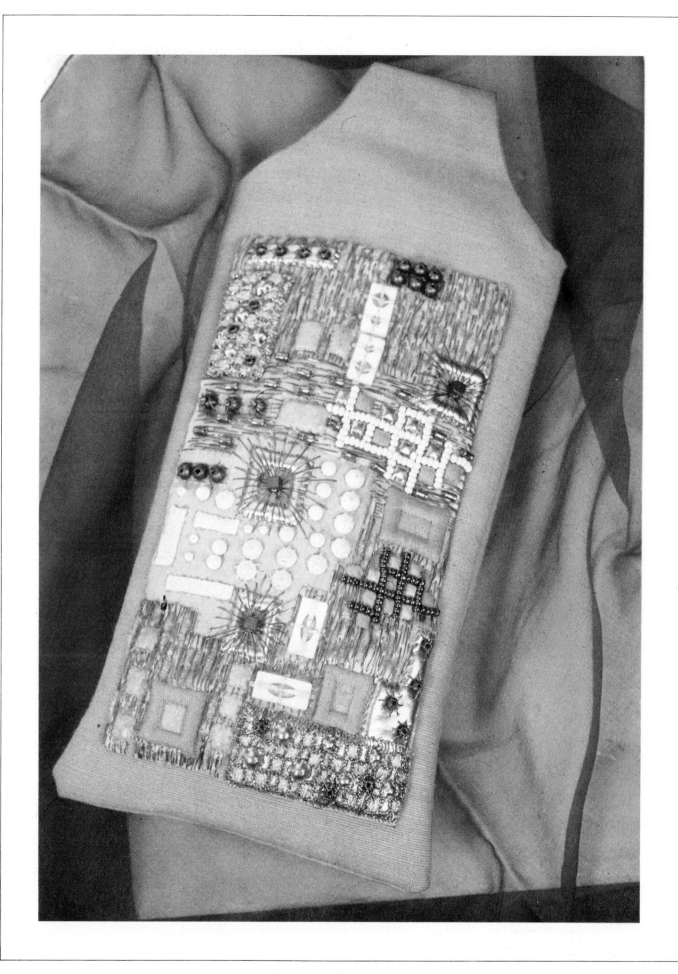

on the design with a pencil. Mount the fabric in a frame.

Using the tracing as a pattern cut out the larger pieces of gold kid (No. 1 in the key), pad with kapok and oversew (overcast) in place. Cut out the larger pieces of lemon kid (4 and 5). Pad the small pieces (5) and sew in place. Sew the biggest piece (4) in place without padding.

Cut out the small squares of lemon kid (2 – in between the gold beads), and oversew in place, placing each one over a square brass stud. Do the same with the lemon kid and gold kid (2 and 3) in between the small white beads. Sew the plastic rectangles in place with groups of 3 stitches using lemon cotton. Then sew on the bright yellow beads round the edges and in the middle as shown.

Cut out the yellow felt squares (6) and white felt rectangles (7) and oversew in place, padding the yellow ones. Oversew a small square of lemon kid in the centre of the yellow felt and gold kid squares. Cut the iridescent braid into 3½-in. and 2½-in. lengths, and oversew in place. Sew 6 of the small round gold-painted wooden beads in place on the braid, using gold thread and taking 8 stitches through the centre of each bead. Sew 11 more small gold beads in place on the braid with a single stitch. Cover with a small circle of gold kid and stitch down. Sew the remainder of these beads in place on the 2 pieces of gold kid as shown.

Sew the 12 large round gold beads in the places shown, with 8 stitches taken

through the centre of each bead, using gold thread. Sew the 3 gold tambour beads on top of one group of 3 as shown. Sew the 3 square gold-painted wooden beads in place on the piece of gold kid (1) and work stitches in gold thread in varying lengths, from the centre of the kid to the outside.

Sew the small gold and white chalk

beads in place by threading several on a length of cotton, taking a long stitch to the length of the threaded beads and securing this with small stitches taken at intervals across the line. Sew on the semi-circular white beads with 8 stitches taken through the centre of each bead,

Right: *Cheshire Cat Cushion.*

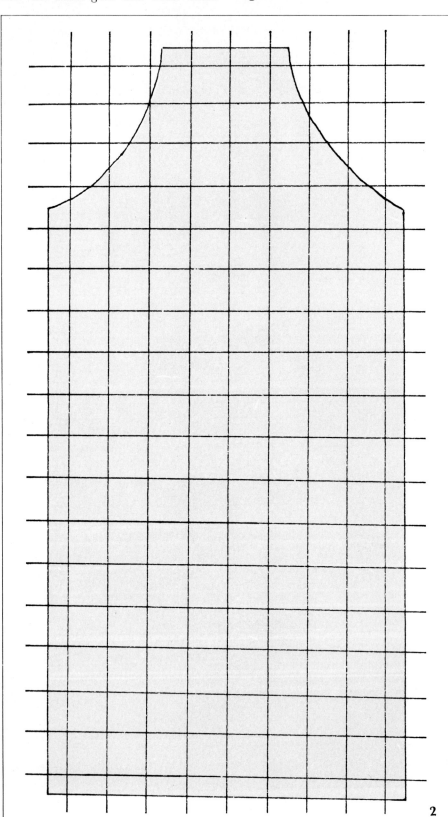

Key for details of
embroidery materials (see page 44)

✳ *large gold wooden bead and gold stitches*
✲ *small gold wooden bead and gold stitches*
◎ *large gold wooden bead with tambour bead on top*
✩ *semi-circular white beads with white stitches through the centre*
○ *medium sized white bead*
⚰ *small white bead with stitches through the centre*
⊕ *bead covered with gold kid*
✴ *square gold wooden bead with gold stitches*
● *small gold beads*
⬭ *white chalk beads*
• *small yellow beads*
/// *iridescent braid*
⊞ *plastic shape and stitches*
1 *gold kid*
2 *lemon kid over the top of a brass stud*
3 *gold kid over the top of a brass stud*
4 *lemon kid*
5 *padded lemon kid*
6 *yellow felt*
7 *white felt*
Both section As are single satin stitch in gold thread and lime green chenille wool.
Section C is single satin stitch in gold thread and gold barrel beads.

46

using white thread. Also with white thread, sew on the small and medium-sized white beads, taking 2 or 3 stitches through the centre of each bead.

Fill in the section 'A's marked on diagram 1, with single satin stitch using wool and gold thread. Vary the stitch length from $\frac{1}{2}$ in. to 1 in. Fill in Section C with single satin stitch using gold thread and incorporating the gold barrel-shaped beads as shown in the illustration.

To make up the bag, cut out 4 pieces in yellow fabric, using the pattern you have drawn. Slipstitch the embroidery in place $1\frac{1}{2}$ ins away from the side and bottom edges of one piece of fabric, padding it slightly with cotton wadding. With right sides together, sew this piece to another pattern piece, along the 3 sides and the top of the handle, allowing a $\frac{1}{2}$-in. seam allowance. Turn the right way out. Sew the other two pieces together in the same way, insert them inside the first 2. Turn in $\frac{1}{4}$-in. turnings along the curved edges and slip stitch the pieces together along these edges.

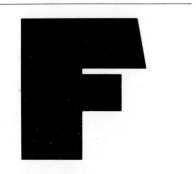

FABRIC CRAFT

Fabric-craft is an all embracing term that covers the use of fabric – any fabric – to make handicraft items. We are fortunate nowadays, that with the many man-made and synthetic fabrics that have been evolved over the last decades, the scope for fabric-craft, in terms of *different* fabrics available, has widened. In working with fabrics, experiment with different kinds – making things using a fabric which might be considered unconventional. Or try mixing fabrics that may appear to be uncomplementary to see the effect they can have upon one another. Bear in mind, however, the use to which the finished article is to be put. If you are making something purely for decoration, the decorative value of the fabric or fabrics is the most important thing to consider, but if you are making practical household articles – tray cloths, table mats, even cushions – it is as well to use fabric which will withstand both constant use and washing, or at least dry cleaning.

Handle each fabric according to its type. Some materials are built for 'rough' handling, but delicate lace fabrics for example, cannot be expected to look their best if they have been pulled about excessively or handled roughly in the making processes. Fabrics prone to fraying will do so more readily if not handled with care. Use an applicable size and type of stitch for each fabric, and if you are using adhesive, make sure you use the correct one for the fabric.

CHESHIRE CAT CUSHION

Materials

$\frac{3}{4}$ yd of 36-ins wide flowered cotton fabric
Black felt, 2×3 ins
6 ins black silk fringe, 1 in. deep
2 yds black cord insertion
$\frac{1}{2}$ yd patent fastening
Wadding and Kapok
Fabric adhesive
Black thread
Thread to match fabric

Method

Enlarge and transfer the cat pattern (1 square = 1 in.) from diagram 1 on to a sheet of folded greaseproof or good quality tissue paper, ruled into 1 in. squares (see page 42). The fold line of the paper should correspond with the straight line of the pattern, which is the centre of the cat. Mark all the cat's features, paws etc. Turn the pattern over and trace the lines through onto the other half of the paper, omitting the tail. Tack the tracing pattern to the right side of the fabric, through a single layer only. Do not cut it out.

Trace the pattern for the nose (see diagram 2) and cut it out in black felt.

Following the lines, and stitching through the paper, outline the inner ears, mouth, paws and tail with narrow black braid – either couching it into position (see page 34), or stitching neatly along the centre of the braid. (Prevent cut ends from fraying with a tiny dab of fabric adhesive). Stitch a $2\frac{1}{2}$-in. length of fringe into place for each eye, and appliqué the nose into position with slip stitch. Stitch cord edge all round outline of cat, the *outer* corded edge of the insertion towards the centre of the cushion. Carefully tear away the tracing, removing any obstinate bits with tweezers.

Cut out cat shape, $\frac{1}{2}$ in. outside insertion cord, and press. To make the back, fold a piece of fabric 20 ins long by 18 ins wide down the centre, and cut. Turn $1\frac{1}{2}$ ins along each centre edge to the wrong side. Stitch patent fastening to each side, then place them together to join, so that the back fabric is in one piece, with the (joined) opening down the centre. (If preferred, use a zip fastener, press studs or a strip of hooks and eyes as used for chair covers, instead of patent fastenings.)

With right sides together, pin the front to the back, matching the centres. Trim back level with the front. Join front and back all round outer edge of cushion with machine stitching, following stitching line of cord edge insertion. Turn to right side and press.

Make an inner cushion the same size as the cover from the wadding (to emphasize shape) and stuff lightly with the Kapok. Alternatively, leave the cat shape as it is and use as a nightdress case.

Right: *Matchbox Magic.*

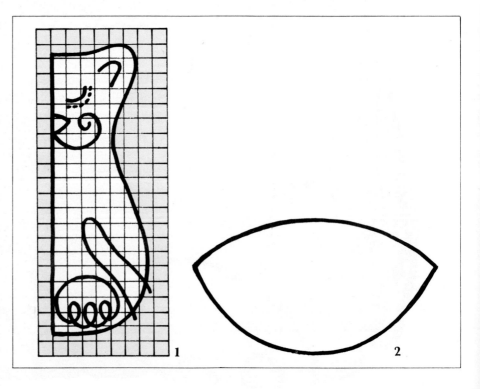

5   6   7   8

MATCHBOX MAGIC

Materials
Boxes of matches
Scraps of assorted fabrics
Narrow ribbon
Stiff cardboard
Fabric adhesive

Method
Group 2, 3 or 4 boxes on a piece of stiff cardboard (diagram 3 shows the different positions of the boxes illustrated in the photograph). When you are happy with the arrangement (make sure it allows you to open all the boxes), draw round the outline of the grouped boxes making sure that they do not move. Cut out the shape with a sharp knife or scissors. Place the shape on another piece of cardboard, draw round it and cut out a second piece.

Using just a smear of adhesive, stick each piece of cardboard to the wrong side of the fabric and then cut out, leaving $\frac{1}{2}$ in. surplus fabric all round. Mitre the corners and clip into the angles (see diagram 4). Fold the excess fabric over and glue it down to the cardboard.

Cut a $2\frac{1}{2}$-in. length of ribbon for each matchbox drawer. Fold the ribbon in half lengthways and glue cut ends inside the boxes so that a looped end protrudes as illustrated.

Glue the matchboxes into position on the wrong side of one piece of covered cardboard. Glue the second piece of covered cardboard on top and press down firmly. Leave the boxes under a weight until quite dry.

BOOK MARKERS

Materials
(given for each marker illustrated on pages 50 and 51, from left to right)
1. 12 ins red satin ribbon, 1 in. wide
26 ins narrow lace trim
2. 12 ins red satin ribbon
9 ins strip lace daisies
2 large lace daisy motifs
3. 12-ins strip dress fabric, 3 ins wide
4. 9-ins strip blue felt, 3 ins wide
Lace motifs
5. $10\frac{1}{2}$-ins strip beige felt, 3 ins wide
Scraps of pink felt
12 ins purple braid trimming
Gilt button
6. $8\frac{1}{2}$-ins strip chamois-leather, $2\frac{1}{2}$ ins wide
Felt-tipped pens
7. 12-ins strip green plaited woollen braid, 2 ins wide
10 ins red rick rack braid
8. $8\frac{1}{2}$-in. strip white evenweave linen
Blue and black embroidery cotton
For all markers: Fabric adhesive

Method
1. Glue narrow lace trim round all edges of the satin ribbon.
2. Glue the strip of lace daisies in the centre of the ribbon. Trim the lace motifs if necessary and glue at either end.
3. Fold the strip of dress fabric in half lengthways and cut either end on a slant. Fold in the raw edges for $\frac{1}{4}$ in. and glue the edges together.
4. Trim the blue felt to a pointed shape

Below: *Chart for cross stitch embroidered marker (8). Without the fringe it measures $7\frac{3}{4}$ ins. Work cross stitch over 2 threads in each direction, and the border in satin stitch.*

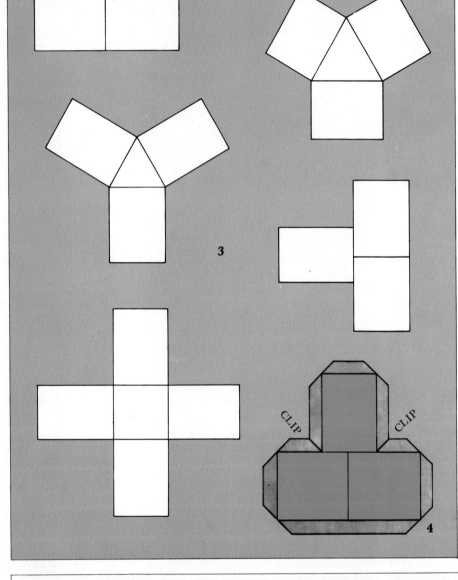

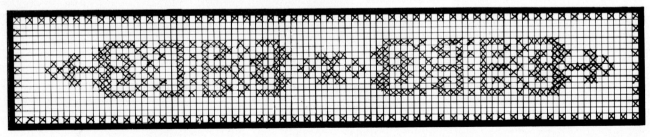

at both ends as shown. Glue lace motifs in place. (Alternatively, stitch the lace motifs in place with small stitches and back the marker with a contrasting coloured felt, glued in place, to hide the stitches.)

5. Trim one end of the felt strip to a point using pinking shears. Trim the remaining 3 sides with pinking shears and fringe the top end by making 5 cuts down for about ¾ in. Cut heart-shaped motifs from pink felt, and glue these, the braid and the button in place.

6. Cut the chamois-leather into the shape shown using pinking shears. Draw on a 'totem-pole' design with felt-tipped pens.

7. Fringe the top and bottom of the plaited woollen braid for about ½ in. Glue rick rack braid down the centre.

8. Following the chart given below, left, embroider the design onto the evenweave linen, in cross stitch. Work satin stitches round the edge of the marker, and fringe the ends top and bottom. (Instructions for how to work cross stitch and satin stitch are given on pages 39 and 34 respectively.)

FAIR ISLE KNITTING

Fair isle knitting, like Aran knitting (see page 11), originated from a small island – Fair Isle – where for years it was used to knit sweaters solely for the people who lived there. Nowadays the distinctive patterns have become internationally popular and are much copied. Fair isle sweaters were originally knitted in many colours with different bands of pattern. As with Aran knitting, each pattern had a meaning, and the knitter used her own taste and imagination to create a garment that was unique. It might start with 'seed' stitch, and be followed by 'water' stitch, intended to water the seed of life. This, in the natural course of events, would be followed by the flower. The help and guidance one needs to go through life was portrayed by an anchor or star motif, and hearts or crosses were often included as a reminder of one's faith. Finally, if the life is well lived, the reward would be the crown of glory and this would decorate the shoulder of the sweater.

Traditionally, Fair isle knitting was worked in beautiful, soft and muted colours, the dyes for which were made from the natural materials found on the island. Shell fish provided the pinks, and seaweed, mosses and lychens made the browns, greens and yellows, so the whole was truly a product of the island.

In some Fair isle knitting patterns, the pattern design is given in chart form, in which each square represents one stitch in the row.

When following a chart, working on two needles in stocking stitch, and starting with a knit row, the first and every odd-numbered row will be read from right to left across the chart. Purl rows and all even-numbered rows will be read from left to right.

If you are working on four needles or a circular needle, then the rounds are all knit rounds and are *all* read from right to left on each round.

Colours may be stranded and for this, you carry the yarn not in use across the back of the work, until it is required.

When working with two colours only, hold one colour in the right hand and the other in the left. It is best to hold the colour to be used most often in the row in the right hand. It becomes simple to take up a stitch or two of the second colour from the left hand, with the point of the right hand needle.

If too many stitches have to be worked in one colour, stranding becomes unsatisfactory. The work can be pulled and the final result be spoilt. In this case, weaving the yarns not in use is the best way. Do this by weaving the colour not in use under that in use for one stitch and over the colour in use on the next stitch.

CHILD'S CAP AND MITTS

Materials

2 balls Double Knitting wool (knitting worsted) in pink (main colour), 1 (1, 2) balls in white and 1 ball in black

1 pair each Nos. 11 (2) and 9 (4) knitting needles

Large eyed needle

Measurements: The cap, unstretched = 15 (16, 17) ins; Mitts, from top of wrist to finger tip = 4½ (5, 5½) ins.

Tension: 6 sts and 8 rows to 1 in. on No. 9 (4) needles.

Abbreviations: See page 5. In addition

W = white, B = black, M = main colour (pink).

Method

Cap: With W and No. 11 (2) needles, cast on 88 (96, 104) sts and work 2 rows k.1, p.1 rib. Change to No. 9 (4) needles and purl 1 row. Inc. 1 st. at end of row. Now begin patt.
1st row: (right side) K.1B, *k.2W, k.3M, k.2W, k.1B, rep. from * to end.
2nd row: P.1W, * p.1B, p.2W, p.1M, p.2W, p.1B, p.1W, rep. from * to end.
3rd row: K.1W, * k.1W, k.1B, k.3W, k.1B, k.2W, rep. from * to end.
4th row: P.1M, * p.2W (p.1B, p.1W) twice, p.1W, p.1M, rep. from * to end.
5th row: K.1M, * k.1M, p.2W, k.1B, k.2W, k.2M, rep. from * to end.
With W purl 2 rows to mark ridge for turn-up. Change to No. 11 (2) needles and p. 1 row. Change to M and work 8 rows in k.1, p.1 rib. Change to No. 9 (4) needles and beg. with a p. row, cont. in M and st. st. and work until 4 (4½, 5) ins. have been completed from turn-up ridge, ending with a p. row. Dec. 1 st. at end of last row.
To shape crown: 1st row: * K.2 tog., k.7 (8, 9), s.k.p.o., rep. from * 8 times. P. 1 row, k. 1 row, p. 1 row.
5th row: * K.2 tog., k.5 (6, 7), s.k.p.o., rep. from * 8 times. Cont. to dec. by 16 sts in same way on every right side row until 24 (16, 24) sts rem., ending after a p. row.
Next row: k.2 tog., to end. Draw yarn through rem. sts and fasten off securely.
Mitts: With M and No. 11 (2) needles, cast on 32 (34, 36) sts and work 15 rows in k.1, p.1 rib.
Next row: P. Change to W and No. 9 (4) needles. Inc. 1 st. at beg. of next row and work 4 rows st.st., beg. with a k. row.
To shape thumb: and to work colour patt. for right-hand mitt:
1st row: K.4 (4, 5) W, k.1B, k.2W, k.3M, k.2W, k.1B, k.3 (4, 4) W, with W, p.u.k., k.1, p.u.k., k.16 (17, 18).
2nd row: P.23 (25, 26) W, p.1B, p.2W, p.1M, p.2W, p.1B, p.5 (5, 6) W.
3rd row: K.6 (6, 7) W, k.1B, k.3W, k.1B, k.5 (6, 6) W, with W, p.u.k., k.3, p.u.k., k.16 (17, 18).
4th row: P.27 (29, 30) W, p.1B, p.1W, p.1B, p.7 (7, 8) W.
5th row: K.5 (5, 6) W, k.1M, p.2W, k.1B, k.2W, k.1M, k.4 (5, 5) W, with W, p.u.k., k.5, p.u.k., k.16 (17, 18) (39, 41, 43) sts.
6th row: In W purl. Cont. in W and work another 2 (2, 4) rows st.st. making 2 sts in same way on k. rows.
To work thumb: Next row: K.25 (26, 29) turn.
Next row: P.9 (9, 11) cast on 2, turn. Work another 12 (14, 16) rows in st.st. on these 11 (11, 13) sts. Draw yarn through rem. sts and fasten off securely.
Hand: With right side facing join in W and k.16 (17, 18) sts on left-hand needle,

turn.
Next row: P.16 (17, 18), pick up and p.2 sts from base of thumb, p. remaining 16 (17, 18) sts.
Next row: K.4 (4, 5) W, k.1B, k.2W, k.3M, k.2W, k.1B, k.21 (23, 24) W. Complete the 5-row colour patt. on sts as set.
For 2nd and 3rd sizes: With W and beg. with p. row, work 5 (7) rows st.st., and then work 5 patt. rows again.
For all sizes: With W. and beg. p. row, cont. in st.st. until work measures 3½ (4, 4½) ins from top of wrist ribbing, ending with p. row.
Top of hand: 1st row: * k.1, k.2 tog., k.11 (12, 13), s.k.p.o., k.1, rep. from * twice.
2nd and alt. rows: P.
3rd row: * K.1, k.2 tog., k.9 (10, 11), s.k.p.o., k.1, rep. from * twice. Now dec. 4 sts on 5th and 7th rows in same way. Cast off on 9th row.
For left-hand mitt: Work as for right hand, but reading instructions for colour patt. rows from end of row to beg.
To make up: Press pieces. Sew seam at back of head of cap. Sew thumb seam and seam round hand of each mitt. Press seams. Trim cap with a pom-pon.

FELT CRAFT

Felt is an ideal material to use in handicraft projects as it does not fray. It is particularly suitable for children to work with as it is easy to handle and can be glued or sewn equally successfully. It is also very attractive – the darker shades are extremely luxurious and deeply coloured, but even the paler shades have a depth and richness of colour found in few other fabrics.
If you are thinking of using felt to make a garment, remember it cannot be washed very successfully and needs to be dry-cleaned. This makes it suitable for bright fashion 'extras' like a special waistcoat, or accessories, such as hats, belts and bags, but it is not really suitable for trousers or a dress! Felt can be used to make a very attractive evening skirt particularly if you choose one of the extra wide ones and make a circular or semi-circular skirt.
Felt can also be used most successfully in home furnishings, for cushions, wall-hangings, to make an appliqué design on nursery curtains, or as a fringed table cover to completely conceal an old circular table – giving it a new lease of life.
You can purchase felt in a number of different forms. It is sold by the yard in various widths and is available from specialist handicraft suppliers, local handicraft shops and departmental stores. It is also possible to buy small 6-in. squares of felt in bright colours, from handicraft and needlecraft specialist

shops and from the haberdashery departments in most large stores. These squares are relatively inexpensive and are ideal for making small flowers or for appliquéing onto larger items.
Sharp dressmaker's scissors are necessary for cutting large pieces of felt, but a small pair of really sharp ones are ideal for cutting more intricate shapes. Pinking shears can be used to cut felt, but are only necessary if you want a decorative edge.
Pins tend to leave a mark in felt, so it is wise to draw round pattern pieces with tailor's chalk and cut out following the chalk line.
Special fabric adhesive can be used for sticking felt, but it can also be hand or machine stitched. Set the tension fairly loosely on the machine, similar to that suitable for sewing a fairly heavy furnishing tweed, otherwise the felt can pucker.
Try using felt in place of the materials suggested for some of the other designs in this book. For example, different felts could be used as the background material for any of the book-markers shown on pages 50–51. The Cheshire Cat cushion shown on page 47 would be very warm and cuddly made in a bright coloured felt.
One point which must be borne in mind when planning to use felt is that it is a thick material. While this can be used to great advantage, it may be a problem if you are planning to use felt on a design requiring fine seaming.
Inevitably felt will give a slightly bulky seam. It is therefore perhaps best used in a design which retains the cut edge. As has already been shown in the aprons, photographed on page 9, felt is an ideal material to use for applique work.

FELT BOOK COVER

Materials
Brown paper (for pattern)
Sufficient felt to wrap round the book, plus 3 ins tuck-in for front and back cover
Contrasting felt for spectacle pocket and trim
Matching or contrasting sewing thread
Fabric adhesive

Method
Measure the book to be covered and make a paper pattern. This should allow ½ in. turning top and bottom and a good 3 in. tuck-in on each side (more if the book is large). Remember the opening and closing of the book places strain on the spine of the book so the finished felt 'jacket' should not fit too tightly. If the book has a dust jacket this can be used as a guide to help make the pattern.
Place pattern on the felt and cut out.

Turn in slightly less than the ½-in. turning top and bottom and machine or hand sew in matching or contrasting thread. Fit 'jacket' round book. Turn in tuck-in and pin in position top and bottom to make sure the fit is not too tight and the book can be easily opened. Oversew top and bottom of front and back of tuck-in to front and back covers, forming pockets into which the book will slip.

Measure spectacles and cut a suitable sized pocket for them from contrasting coloured felt. Stick or stitch in place on the front of the cover.

Cut a trimming motif, such as a flower from felt and stick or stitch it in place. Alternative trimming could be the book owner's initials, a butterfly, leaves, hearts, fruit etc. Another idea is to design something which ties in with the book title.

FELT FLOWERS

Materials
Scraps of green, white, yellow, purple, orange, violet, pink, cream, grey and black felt. (Use left-over scraps or buy 6 in. squares)
Fabric adhesive
Sewing thread to tone with felt
Wire for stiffening

Method
A basic method can be used to make stems, leaves and flowers for all the felt flowers illustrated. This can then be adapted to create the various different kinds.

To make stems: Cut a strip of green felt 4½ ins long by ¾ in. wide. Roll it into a tubular stem shape and oversew along the edge. To make the stem more rigid, insert a piece of soft wire into the tubular stem, and then sew up the bottom. This enables the stem to be bent into any desired shape.

To make leaves: Cut out 2 leaf shapes (see diagram overleaf for individual shapes) and stick them together with fabric adhesive. Make sure the edges are firmly stuck. Oversew approximately 1 in. at the base of the leaf to the bottom of the stem.

To make basic flower: Cut the sepal shapes and petals according to flower required (see diagram and caption). Cut a small cross through the felt in the middle of each sepal shape and each set of petals. Push the petals and then the sepal shapes gently onto the stem. Secure all pieces to the stem with a few small stitches, or if preferred, stick in position.

Daisy: Use white felt for petals, one or two shades of yellow for sepals, and

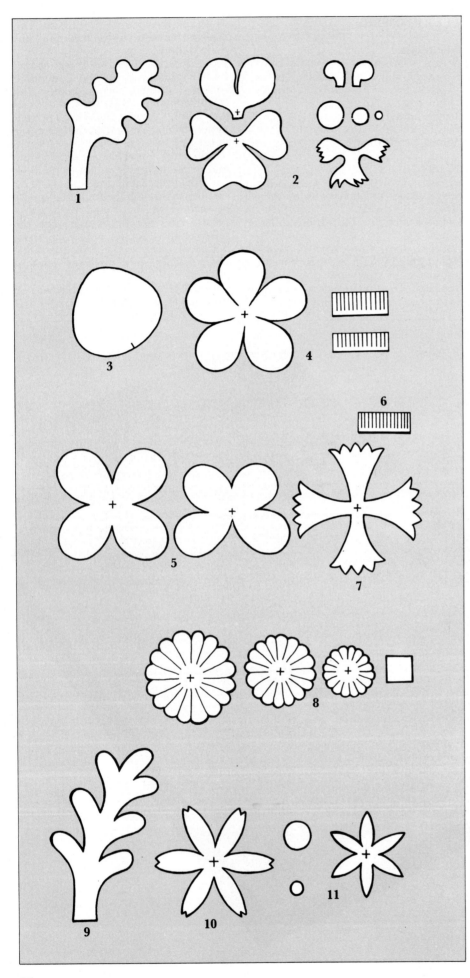

green felt for the leaves. Make following the basic instructions.

Pansy: Use shades of purple, violet and pink felt for the petals, cream, yellow and black for the centre and green for the leaves and stem. Make following the basic instructions.

Kingcup: Use yellow felt for the petals, grey, black and pale yellow for the centre and green for the leaves and stem. Make as the basic flower.

Anemone: Use pink and purple felt for the petals, black for the centre and green for the leaves and stem. Make as before.

Marigold: Use orange or vivid yellow felt for the petals, and centre, and green for the leaves and stem. Make as before. These designs can be adapted to make many other flowers.

FINISHING TOUCHES

Adding 'finishing touches' to hand-made articles and garments can make the difference between them looking professional or 'home-made'. Clothes for example, can be made to look extremely expensive and shop-bought, simply by the addition of decorative details such as a braid trim or an embroidered motif. Knitted garments are often greatly improved if they are finished off with a woollen fringe or

Left: *Leaf, petal and sepal shapes for flowers illustrated above. 1 and 2: Leaf and petal shapes for pansy. 3 and 4: Leaf and petal shapes for kingcup. 5 and 6: Petal and sepal shapes for anemone. 7: Leaf shape for anemone. 8: Petal shape for marigold. 9: Leaf shape for daisy and marigold. 10: Petal shape for daisy. 11: Sepal shape for pansy, kingcup, daisy and marigold.*

some tassels and home furnishings take on a luxury look with the help of subtly blending trimmings.

Whatever finishing touch you choose to give to an item you have made, make sure that if you mean the colours to match, they do so exactly. Likewise, if you want the trimming to provide a contrast, make sure it looks deliberate and definite. Far from improving an item, poorly matched or blended trimmings will make it look shoddy and unprofessional.

For the same reason, extra care should be taken in the making of finishing touches (in the case of tassels, fringes, pompons etc.) and in attaching them to the article. Insecure and clumsy-looking stitches will certainly not give the 'finished' effect you are seeking to achieve.

Below are some suggestions for materials to use and ways of adding finishing touches to bought or home-made items.

Braid

Braid can be used simultaneously to decorative and functional use. Using it to bind the raw edge of a garment or household article so that no facing is required is functional, but, at the same time, it provides an attractive and decorative finish.

To apply braid in this way, fold it along its length, with the wrong sides together, just off the centre line, so that one side is slightly wider than the other (see diagram 1). Press the braid to define the crease, then use it to encase the raw edges of the item. The widest side should be on the wrong side of the item, and the narrowest side on the right side. Pin or baste it in place. Then machine stitch on the right side of the item, close to the edge of the braid, through all thicknesses (see diagram 2). By placing the slightly wider side of the braid on the wrong side of the article, you can ensure that your stitching will encase all thicknesses. If

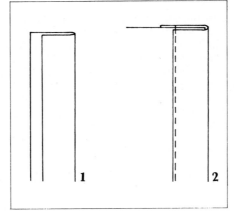

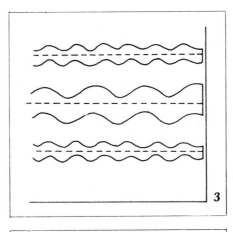

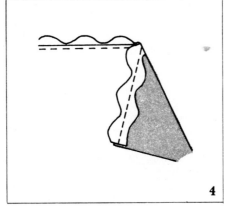

the braid has to be continued round a corner, stitch to within 1 in. of the corner and then form a mitre on both the right and wrong sides by folding under the excess triangle of fabric. Continue stitching, pivoting the machine through 90 degrees at the corner.

Rick rack braid

This is a very simple braid that has been popular for many years, and has great value in adding finishing touches to all manner of things. Its many uses include decorative application to children's and adult's clothes – round the hem of a skirt for example, or to pick out design details such as pockets and yokes. It has significant home use too, for such things as trimming the edges of curtains, tablecloths and bedspreads. It can look particularly effective if several widths and harmonizing colours are used in this way in conjunction with one another (see diagram 3).

To apply rick rack braid, pin or baste it in position and straight stitch along the centre through the braid and the underneath fabric.

It can also be used as a decorative edging for the very bottom of an article. In this case, turn the edge of the fabric which it will be trimming to the wrong side and press. Pin the braid onto the edge of the fabric, either overlapping on the right or wrong side (see diagram 4), depending upon the effect you want to achieve. If you pin it to the wrong side, the points of one edge of the braid only will be visible from the right side. Machine stitch the braid in place close to the edge of the fabric, from the right side.

Scallops

This is a very attractive finish that can be used to equal advantage for clothes or home furnishings. Scallops may be cut from matching or harmonizing fabric to the item they are to trim.

Cut out a tissue paper pattern for scallops to ensure they are even and then transfer the outline to the fabric, by using dressmaker's carbon paper and a tracing wheel (see page 43).

Alternatively you can place the tissue pattern piece over the work and actually stitch along the line on the tissue through to the fabric and its facing. This latter method will mean that you are unable to use the pattern again, as it must be torn away from either side of the stitching afterwards.

It is a good idea to transfer the scallop line to the facing, rather than the top fabric. Stitch along this line through both thicknesses using small machine stitches to form a smooth curved line (see diagram 5). At the points, take one or two small stitches straight across before commencing the next curve. This will make it easier to turn the scallops

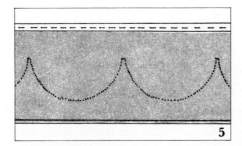

5

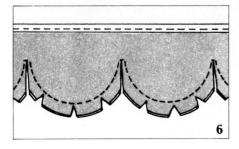

6

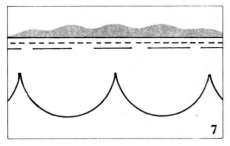

7

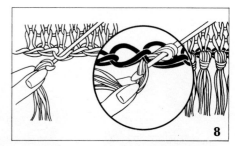

8

through to the right side on completion. When you have finished stitching all the scallops, trim the seam allowance to about $\frac{1}{4}$ in. and then cut notches round the curves so it will lie flat. Clip right up to the stitching at the points (see diagram 6), taking care not to clip the stitches. (If you are using interfacing between the fabric and its facing, trim it very close to the stitching line, then trim round the curves and notch them.) Turn the facing to the wrong side and press out the edges of the scallops first on the facing side and then on the front of the item. To make sure that this edge will not roll after the item has been laundered or dry-cleaned, make small prick stitches through from the facing to the seam allowance making sure that the garment fabric is not caught-in (see diagram 7). The facing now forms a hem and can be hemmed in the usual way.

Tassels and Pompons

Tassels and pompons, can be used to add the finishing touches to a variety of household furnishings and clothes. They can be made from many different types of thread and yarn, to harmonize with the fabric of the articles for which they are required.

Tassels make attractive finishing touches for such clothes as hats and scarves, and can also be used effectively to trim the corners of cushions for example.

To make a tassel, cut a piece of cardboard the length you wish the finished tassel

to be. Wind yarn round the cardboard – the number of times will depend on how 'thick' you want the finished tassel. Thread a large-eyed needle with a length of matching yarn. Pass it through the loops at the top of the cardboard several times and secure it, but do not cut yarn.

Cut end of the wound yarn at the bottom of the cardboard. Pass the needle through the top to about 1 in. below the cut ends. Take another length of matching yarn and wind it round the top of tassel, about $\frac{1}{4}$ of total length from top. Tie firmly and with the needle, pass the ends through to join the cut ends. Trim ends.

Although pompons could be made from any yarn, they are most effective made from wool, and they make attractive finishing touches to add to scarves and hats.

To make a pompon, cut 2 circles of firm cardboard. The diameter should be that required for the finished pompon. Cut a circle out of the centre of each piece and place the circles together. Wind yarn through the centre hole, taking it round and round both pieces of cardboard until the centre hole is completely filled up.

Thread matching yarn through a large eyed needle. Cut the loops of yarn between the 2 circles. Bind yarn in needle tightly between the circles, round the centre of the cut lengths of yarn. Tie very firmly. Remove the cardboard circles and trim the pompon evenly.

Twisted cords

Cords will make belts or ties to thread through bags. Really thick ones with tassels will make smart ties for curtains. To make a cord, cut several lengths of yarn about 3 times the length required for the finished cord. (You will need sufficient to make half the thickness you want the finished cord to be.) Secure one end firmly, hold the other end, and twist it until it forms a firm, tight cord. Fold in half and allow the two sides to twist together from the centre. Tie a knot in each end and trim with a tassel. two-coloured cord can be made in the same way. It looks neatest if the original strands are half one colour and half the other, the two colours being tied in the middle. When the twisted strands are allowed to run together, the colours will appear to be striped neatly.

Fringes

Fringes make some of the most effective finishing touches. Clothes, cushions, bedspreads, lampshades and many other items, can have their appearances greatly improved by a fringe worked in a harmonizing, or contrasting, colour. They can be any thickness that you care to make. Cut lengths of yarn a little more than twice the length of the re-

quired fringe. Take 2 or more strands, according to the thickness of fringe you want to make. Fold in half and with a crochet hook, draw the fold through the edge which is to be decorated (see diagram 8).

Draw the ends through the loop of the fold and pull tight.

For a fancier fringe use longer strands. Divide each individual tassel into 2 equal parts. Start from one end of fringe and knot together the second half of first tassel and first half of second together, about 1 in. below tassel loops. Continue to end, keeping row of knots level. On next row, 1 in. below knots, take all the alternate halves of tassels and knot in the same way.

FLORENTINE EMBROIDERY

Florentine embroidery is worked on a canvas background, in straight stitches, which can be arranged to form a variety of patterns. Yarn colours should be carefully chosen to achieve the brilliant effect which is typical of this kind of embroidery. Traditionally, the colours range from light to dark in a closely related scheme.

The spectacles case pattern (right) is worked in a zig-zag formation, called 'flame' and is one of the basic Florentine or Bargello patterns.

SPECTACLE CASE

Materials

12×12 ins single weave canvas, 16 threads to 1 in.

1 skein tapisserie wool in each of following colours:
Cream
Sand
Amber
Orange
Brown
Maroon

12×12 in brown lining silk

1 skein stranded embroidery thread in Cinnamon

Tapestry needle

Embroidery needle

Blotting paper

Right: *Florentine Spectacle Case.*

Method

Draw out the shape of the case (see diagram 1, 2 squares = 1 in.) and trace it on to the canvas, using either dark coloured water colour paint and a brush or a felt-tipped pen. Choose any of the colours for the foundation row and following the chart (see diagram 2) work one row of the pattern right across the canvas from side to side of the case. Work each stitch over 3 threads of the canvas in the way shown in diagram 3.

You will find that you will work just over three repeats of the basic pattern shown in diagram 2. When the foundation row is completed, work the rest of the pattern, changing to the next colour for each row. The flame pattern illustrated uses the yarn colours in the following order: cream, sand, amber, orange, brown and maroon.

When you reach the edges of the outlined shape you will find that, to follow the curves, you may have to work over 2 or even a single thread. This is acceptable, as long as you keep to the order of the colours in the pattern.

When you have completed the embroidery, stretch the canvas as follows: lay 2 or 3 thicknesses of blotting paper on a board and dampen the paper thoroughly. Place the embroidery face upwards on the dampened paper and using drawing pins, pin the work to the board, working from the centre of the top edge and outwards. Leave until the paper has dried out.

Unpin the canvas and trim the excess canvas away to within ½ in. of the embroidery. Fold the turnings to the wrong side and baste. It may be necessary to clip into the top edge curve to make the canvas fold more easily. Make sure that no unworked canvas shows on the folded edge – if stitches have been missed out, this is the point at which they should be worked. Cut the lining fabric to match the trimmed canvas size and turn the ½ in. turnings to the wrong side. Press and then baste the lining to the wrong side of the canvas work, matching straight edges.

Slip stitch all round.

Fold the spectacle case down the middle, matching the sides and oversew the long side and across the bottom with tiny, neat stitches.

Finish off these edges with oversewing stitch, worked in the stranded embroidery thread.

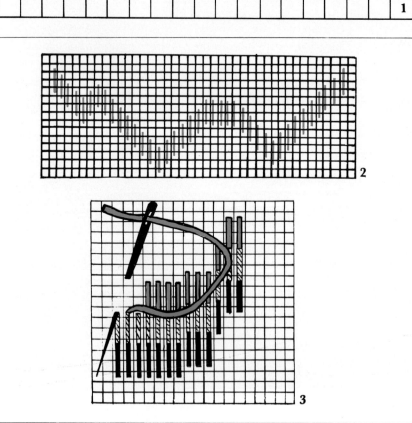

Spectacles case

1

2

3

GARTER STITCH

Garter stitch is the simplest knitting stitch to do. It is the name for 'plain' or 'knit' stitch, which is always the first stitch to be mastered when learning to knit.

QUICK-KNIT JUMPER

Instead of the usual method for knitting a jumper from waist to neck, this one is knitted in one piece from sleeve to sleeve. Fastening at the back, it is easy to put on a small baby.

Right: *Quick-knit Jumper.*

Materials

1 (2, 2) 50-gr. balls of Pingouin Super-bebe (Fingering 3-ply)

1 pair each of No. 10 (3) and 12 (1) knitting needles

5 small buttons

¾ yd narrow ribbon

Embroidery wool (yarn)

Measurements: To fit a 16 (18, 20) in. chest.

Tension: 7 sts and 13 rows to 1 in. over No. 10 (3) needles.

Abbreviations: See page 5.

Method

Begin at Centre Back: With No. 10 (3) needles cast on 39 (45, 51) sts for Left Back and work in g.st. for 22 rows.

Next row: (neck edge) K.7, k. twice into next st., k. to end.

Next row: K.

Rep. last 2 rows until there are 51 (59, 67) sts ending at neck edge. K. 12 (16, 20) rows straight for shoulder.

** Cast on 23 (25, 27) sts for sleeve, k. these 23 (25, 27) sts, then k. across 23 (25, 27) more sts, sl. and leave last 28 (34, 40) sts on a spare needle.

Work on the 46 (50, 54) sleeve sts for 50 (54, 58) rows, k.2 tog. at each end of last row.

44 (48, 52) sts on needle.

Change to No. 12 (1) needles and work in k.2, p.2 rib for 10 rows. Cast off in rib.

Return to shoulder edge of 23 (25, 27) cast on sleeve sts, and with right side facing, pick up and k. these 23 (25, 27) sts, then k. across 28 (34, 40) sts on spare needle.

Next row: K. to last st. pick up end st. from first g.st. ridge on shoulder and k. it t.b.l. tog. with last st. on needle.

Next row: K.

Rep. last 2 rows (to form shoulder) until 7 (9, 11) sts have been picked up and worked tog. with previous st., and ending at neck edge.

Next row: K.7, k.2 tog., k. to end.

Next row: K.

Rep. last 2 rows until 39 (45, 51) sts rem. and ending at neck edge **.

Cont. thus:

1st and alt. rows: K.

2nd row: K.29 (35, 41), p.8, k.2.

4th row: K.27 (33, 39), p.8, k.4.

6th row: K.25 (31, 37), p.8, k.6.

8th row: K.23 (29, 35), p.8, k.8.

10th row: As 6th row.

12th row: As 4th row.

14th row: As 2nd row.

K.2 rows.

Next row: K.7, k. twice into next st., k. to end.

Next row: K.

Rep. last 2 rows until there are 51 (59, 67) sts ending at neck edge.

K.14 (18, 22) rows straight, then rep. from ** to **.

K.18 rows straight.

Next row: K.6, * y.r.n., k.2 tog. (for buttonhole), k.7 (9, 11). Rep. from *

twice more, y.r.n., k.2 tog., k. to end.

K. 3 rows. Cast off.

Neckband: Using No. 10 (3) needles and with right side of work facing, pick up and k.82 (90, 98) sts round neck.

Next row: * P.2, k.2. Rep. from * to last 2 sts, p.2.

Next row: * K.2, y.r.n., p.2 tog. Rep. from * to last 2 sts, k.2.

Work 3 more rows in rib. Cast off in rib.

Welt: Using No. 10 (3) needles and with right side of work facing, pick up and k.118 (134, 150) sts round lower edge.

Next row: * P.2, k.2. Rep. from * to last 2 sts, p.2.

Next row: * K.2, p.2. Rep. from * to last 2 sts, k.2.

Rep. these 2 rows twice more, then 1st row again.

Next row: K.2, p.2 tog., y.r.n. (for

buttonhole) rib to end.

To make up: work 3 more rows in rib then cast off in rib. Do not press. Join sleeve seams. Sew on buttons. Thread ribbon through holes at neck, draw up to required size and tie in a bow.

HOODED PLAY JUMPER

Materials

9 (10, 11) 50 gr. balls of Robin Vogue red Double Double wool (Knitting Worsted or Bulky)

1 ball each of blue and yellow as above

1 pair each of No. 5 (8) and 7 (6) knitting needles

No. 7 (G/6) crochet hook

2 buttons

Right: *His and Her Tidy Bags.*

Measurements: To fit a 22 (24, 26) in. chest.

Tension: 4 sts to 1 in. over g.st. on No. 5 (8) needles.

Abbreviations: See page 5. In addition: R = red; B = blue; Y = yellow.

Method

Back: Using No. 5 (8) needles and R, cast on 48 (52, 56) sts and work in g.st. until back measures 7 (8½, 9½) ins from beg.

Shape Armholes: Cast off 6 (6, 7) sts at beg. of next 2 rows, 36 (40, 42) sts *. Cont. straight until armhole measures 4½ (5, 5½) ins from beg.

Shape Shoulders: Cast off 5 sts at beg. of next 2 rows and 4 (5, 5) sts on next 2 rows. Leave rem. 18 (20, 22) sts on a holder.

Front: Work as Back to *, then work 2 (4, 4) rows straight.

Divide for Front Opening: Next row: K.16 (18, 19), cast off 4, k. to end. Work on last set of sts, ** work straight until armhole measures 3½ (4, 4½) ins ending at front edge.

Shape Neck: Cast off 3 (4, 4) sts at beg. of next row and 3 (3, 4) sts on next alt. row, then dec. 1 st. at same edge on next alt. row 9 (10, 10) sts. Work straight until knitting measures same length as back to beg. of shoulder shaping ending at armhole edge.

Shape Shoulder: Cast off 5 sts at beg. of next row, then work 1 row. Cast off rem. sts.

Return to other sts, rejoin yarn at inner edge to rem. sts and work to match first side working from ** to end.

Sleeves: Begin at shoulder. Using No. 5 (8) needles and B, cast on 36 (40, 44) sts and work in g.st. for 1¾ (1¾, 2) ins. Place marker at edge of last row. Work 4 (6, 8) rows more, then dec. 1 st. each end of next and every foll. 8th row until 24 (26, 28) sts rem. Work straight until sleeves measures 7½ (9, 10½) ins from marker – or required length. Cast off.

Crochet Edgings: Join shoulder, side and sleeve seams. Using No. 7 (G/6) crochet hook, with wrong side facing and R, work round lower edges of back, front and sleeves as follows:

1st round: 1 d.c. (s.c.) into each st., join with a s.s.

2nd round: In B as 1st round.

3rd round: In Y as 1st round.

4th round: As 2nd round.

5th round: As 1st round. Fasten off.

Front Bands: Using No. 7 (G/6) crochet hook, R, and with wrong side facing, work 4 rows of d.c. (s.c.) turning each time with 1 ch. – along right front edge. Fasten off.

Work left front to match but making 2 buttonholes in 2nd row by working 1 ch. instead of a d.c. (s.c.), 3 sts in from each edge. In 3rd row work a d.c. (s.c.) into the 1 ch. sp. Stitch down side edge at base, left overlapping right.

Hood: Using No. 7 (6) needles and R and with right side facing and omitting frontbands, pick up and k.12 (13, 13) sts from right front neck, k.18 (20, 22) sts from back neck and 12 (12, 13) sts from left front neck. 42 (45, 48) sts. Work 4 rows g.st. Change to No. 5 (8) needles.

Next row: K.1, inc. in next st., * k.2, inc. in next st. Rep. from * to last st., k.1. 56 (60, 64) sts.

Work straight in g.st. until work measures 7 (8, 8½) ins or length required. Cast off. Fold cast off edge in half and join on wrong side.

Hood Edging: With right side facing, and R, work crochet edging as before but work in rows, cutting each colour at end of row and beg. all rows at same edge. Work last row across each side edge for a neat finish.

To make up: Press lightly on wrong side using a warm iron over a damp cloth. Set in sleeves, sewing the part above marker to cast off armhole sts. Cut 5 in. lengths of each colour and, alternating colours, knot a fringe (see page 58) all round lower edge, along join of hood and down centre of back hood to neck. Turn back hood edging and tack down at each side of neck edge.

Work the cross stitch embroidery 1 st. in width and 1 g.st. ridge in depth. Mark centre 2 sts between front band and first row of crochet edging in B. Work 4 crosses at centre, i.e. 2 rows of 2 in B, then using Y and leaving 2 g.st. ridges above and below and 2 sts at each side, work '1 box' of cross stitches around centre and another 'box' in B at same intervals as before, as shown in photograph. (Instructions for how to work cross stitch are given on page 39.) Sew on buttons.

GRAFTING

Grafting is the method used in knitting for joining two sets of stitches without a ridge. When finished the line joined appears as knit stitches. This is useful for the toes of socks and can also be used for the shoulders of sweaters.

Materials

Pieces of knitting to be grafted, (sts still on needles, *not* cast off).

Large-eyed needle

Yarn, as used in knitting

Method

To graft a toe, divide the number of stitches equally between 2 knitting needles. For shoulders of sweaters place the wrong sides of the back and front together, with the points of the needles to the right hand side and the end of yarn on the back needle at the right. Thread yarn into a large-eyed needle.

* Insert yarn needle purlwise through loop of the first stitch on front knitting needle but do not slip this stitch off. Then insert yarn needle knitwise through the first stitch on the back needle but do not slip off.

Insert yarn needle again knitwise through the first stitch on the front needle and slip it off. Insert the needle purlwise through second stitch on front needle, but do not slip it off. Now insert yarn needle purlwise through first stitch on back needle and slip this off knitting needle, then insert yarn needle through second stitch on back needle knitwise and do not slip it off.

Repeat from * until all stitches are worked off.

Grafting in k.1, p.1, rib: This will be needed if an unbroken line of stitches is to remain in ribbing joined by this method.

You will need a set of four needles with points at both ends.

Take the first piece of ribbing and slip all the knit stitches on to one needle and hold at front of work. Slip the purl stitches on to a second needle and hold at back of work (see diagram 1). Arrange the stitches from second piece of ribbing in the same way.

Graft the two sets of knit stitches as given for ordinary grafting (see diagram 2). Turn work to the other side and the purl stitches on the right side will have become knit stitches. Deal with them as before.

1 *Knit stitches on one needle and purl stitches on the second to prepare a piece of ribbing for grafting.*

2 *Two sets of ribbed stitches placed together and the grafting of the knit stitches on one side.*

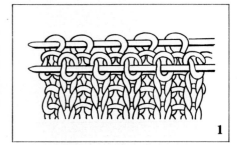

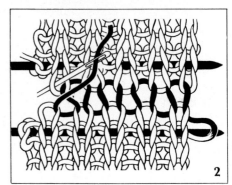

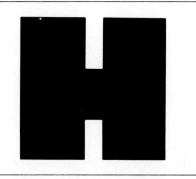

HIS AND HERS

'HER' TIDY BAG

Materials

27 ins of 36-in. wide patterned cotton
  without vertical design
3 yds bias binding
Matching thread
Shirring elastic
Plastic-covered hanger

Method

Cut 1 20-in. strip, and 2 8-in. strips, all 27 ins long from cotton fabric. With bias binding and matching thread, bind 1 long edge of each of the 2 smaller strips. Gather the unbound long edge of each of these strips to a length of 20 ins. Turn in a small hem along the unbound edges and machine one strip along lower (20 in.) edge of the 27 in. long strip, for the lower pocket. Machine the other strip 10 ins up from the lower edge for the upper pocket. Thread shirring elastic through the binding of each pocket-top. Pin and tack sides of pockets to sides of main strip, and bind the two long edges through the pockets and the main fabric. Work lines of stitching on pockets to give separate compartments. Turn in a hem along the top edge of the bag and machine over coat hanger.

'HIS' TIDY BAG

Materials

46 ins of 48 in. furnishing fabric
3½–4 yds braid
Matching thread
Wooden coat hanger

Method

Cut a strip 20 × 40 ins, 2 pockets 20 × 8 ins, 1 6-in. square and 1 further piece 6 × 10 ins, all from the furnishing fabric. Bind one long top edge of each of the pocket strips, and one short end of the long main strip, using the braid. Fold up this last bound edge to form the lowest 8 in. pocket and pin in place; pin the other 2 pockets immediately above, the lower edge of each coinciding with top edge of the pocket below; then pin in place the narrow and square pockets immediately above third long pocket (see diagram below for fabric lay-out). This should leave just sufficient material to fold over the bar of a wooden coat hanger. Machine the lower edges of all pockets in place, and the centre edges of the 2 smaller top pockets. Pin the side pocket edges to match the side edges of main piece as for woman's tidy bag (the man's has no gathering as the material is stronger). Bind the two long edges. Neaten ends. Sew top edge over bar of coat hanger.

INTERFACINGS

Interfacings are most commonly used in garment or dress-making. They comprise a layer of fabric which is placed between the facing and the wrong side of the main fabric of the garment to provide crispness of line and shape, and extra strength or support.

General points to remember when choosing interfacings, are that they should never be heavier than the main fabric, and should have similar properties to the fabric they are interfacing. It is important, for example, to use a washable interfacing if the fabric of the garment is also washable.

Woven Interfacings

These have 'grain' and should be cut either with or against this grain, according to the pattern layout you are using. They include:

Batiste: used to interface dresses, blouses and other garments made of lightweight fabrics. It should be shrunk before using.

Calico (unbleached): adds substance without stiffness, and can be used to back a loosely-woven fabric. It also needs to be shrunk before use.

Canvas: available in stiff and soft finishes. The stiff type is suitable to interface heavyweight fabrics such as those used to make jackets and coats; the softer type is suitable for lightweight fabrics. It can only be dry cleaned.

Lawn: is washable, and suitable for cotton and other washable lightweight fabrics.

Net: used to give backing to sheer fabrics. Synthetic nets are washable but others will need to be dry cleaned.

Taffeta: gives a crisp finish to medium-weight fabrics and is particularly good for evening dresses and skirts for this reason. Available in different types – some are washable, others need to be

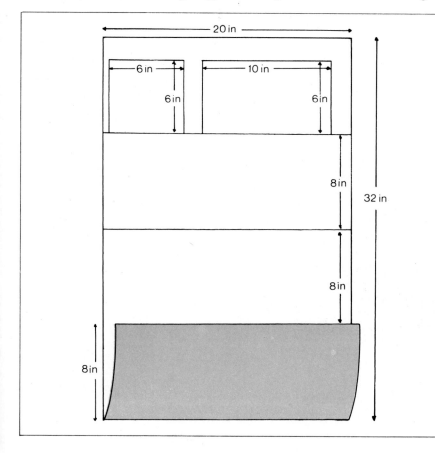

dry cleaned.
Organdie: gives a crisp finish to lightweight fabrics. It is washable.

Non-woven interfacings

These have no grain and can therefore
be cut in any direction.
Lightweight sew-in: is suitable for all light
and mediumweight fabrics where a
soft stiffening is required. It is washable.
It can be used in strips to ensure a permanent knife edge appearance to a pleat
if cut to the length of the pleat, less the
hem, and machined to the pleat backing.
Mediumweight sew-in: used with medium
and heavier weight fabrics, and when a
firmer stiffening is required. Washable.
To apply non-woven sew-in interfacings,
cut interfacing to the same size as the
pattern piece and place it in position
on the wrong side of the fabric pattern
piece. Baste round the edges and trim
the interfacing close to the stitching.
Proceed with the next stage.
Soft iron-on: used on lightweight fabrics
for small areas of stiffening only – e.g.
collars, cuffs and pockets. Not advisable
for use with silk, some synthetic fabrics
and pure white fabrics. It is washable.
Firm iron-on: for use on medium and
heavyweight fabrics in small areas, e.g.
belts and hat brims. It is also washable.
To apply an iron-on non-woven interfacing, cut the interfacing to approximately $\frac{1}{16}$ in. smaller all round, than the
size of the pattern piece. Lay the
powdered or rough side of the interfacing
to the wrong side of the fabric. Fuse
together with a hot iron, preferably
steam, pressed directly on the smooth
side of the interfacing. Make sure you
press evenly all over, and then leave it
for a few minutes to cool before con-
tinuing to make-up the garment.

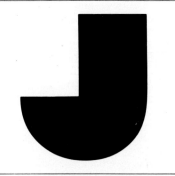

JEWELLERY

Attractive jewellery can be made by
imaginative stringing of different colour-

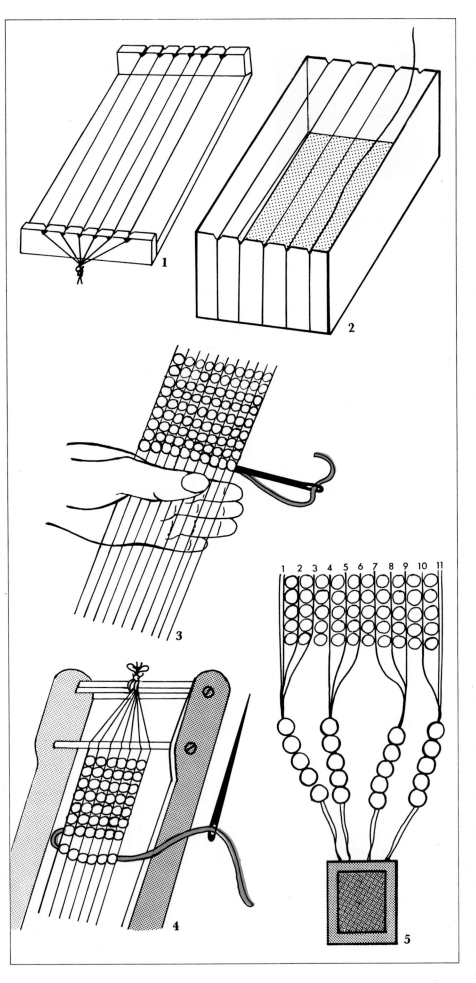

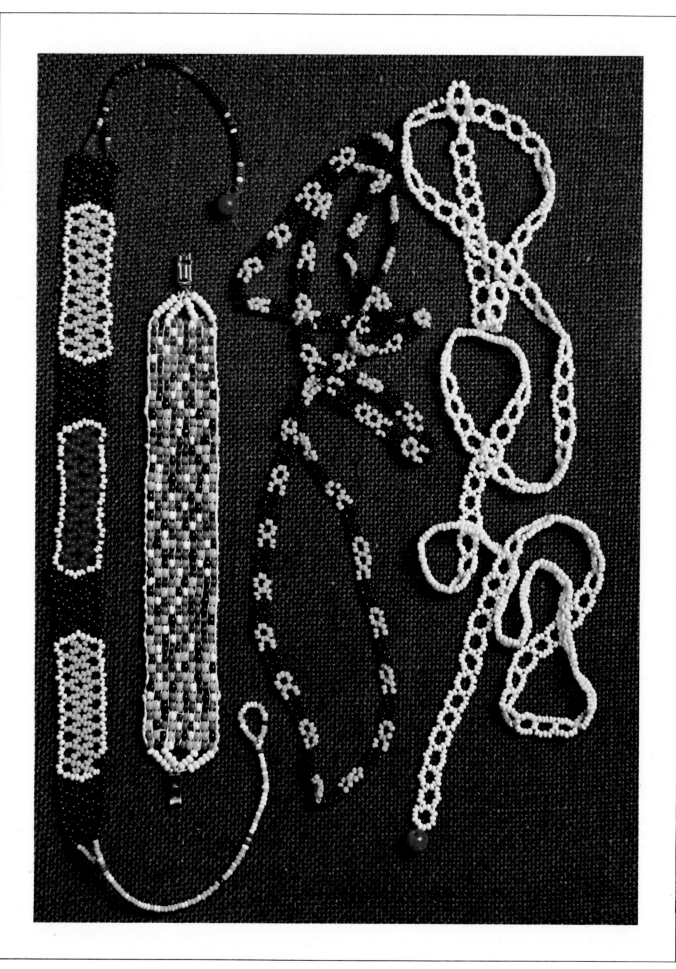

ed beads, or by using a simple loom. This is another popular revival of an old and traditional handicraft.

Looms for bead weaving may be purchased or made at home using small blocks of wood or a strong cardboard box (see diagrams 1 and 2). The threads that lie lengthwise across the looms are called the 'warp' threads and the beads will lie between them.

Main points to remember in bead weaving are that the distance between the warp threads should be the same as the width of the beads to be used; that when threading up the loom, there must always be one more warp thread than there are beads in the pattern, and that there should be one extra thread on either outside edge to give strength to the sides of the weaving. These two threads are always used together.

The Woven Bracelet is worked in a random design.

WOVEN BRACELET

Materials

Assorted embroidery beads in white and 7 different tones of blue and green
Linen beading thread
Beading needle
Bracelet clasp (jeweller's findings)
Loom (see under 'Method')

Method

Use either a bought or home-made loom to make the bracelet. Home-made looms are shown in diagrams 1 and 2. To make the loom in diagram 1 (for weaving this bracelet specifically), glue 2 small strips of wood either end of a longer piece. The strips must be at least 7½ ins apart. Make 11 notches across these strips, the same distance apart as the width of the beads. To make the loom in diagram 2, you will need a cardboard box, not less than 7½ ins long. Make 11 notches at opposite ends, again the same distance apart as the width of the beads.

Thread up your loom with 13 warp threads at least 13 ins long (i.e. the finished length of the bracelet – 7 ins – plus 3 ins extra at either end). Remember to thread 2 warp threads together at either outside edge.

Thread the beading needle with thread. Tie the end to the double thread on the left side and weave 4 rows without beads to strengthen the weaving. (Do not use too long a thread or it will become tangled). Finish on the left. Thread 10 beads in random colours through the needle and push down onto the thread. Place the thread with the beads under the warp threads so that a bead lies between each of the warp threads.

Press the beads up between the warp threads with a finger of your free hand (see diagram 3) and pass the needle from right to left, back through the holes in each bead. This secures them between

the warp threads (see diagram 4). Pull the thread tightly (but not so tight it will distort the straight edge of the weaving). Continue in this way, weaving rows in random colours until the bracelet measures 7 ins.

Work 2 rows of weaving without beads. Take the working thread back through the last row but one of the weaving. Knot off and cut the thread. Lift the warp threads off the loom and cut them back to 3 ins at either end if necessary. Thread warp threads 2 and 3 back through the threads so that they lie alongside the doubled outside threads. Starting at one end, thread the outside 4 threads through 5 white beads. Working in groups of 3 threads, thread 5 white beads on warp threads 4, 5 and 6; 7, 8 and 9; and 10 and 11 (see diagram 5), so you have 4 lots of 5 threaded white beads. Knot the end of the thread onto one part of the bracelet fastening. Work the other end of the bracelet in exactly the same way.

The 3 necklaces below, are all made without the use of a loom.

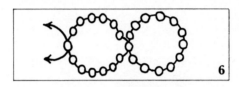

6

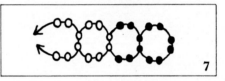

7

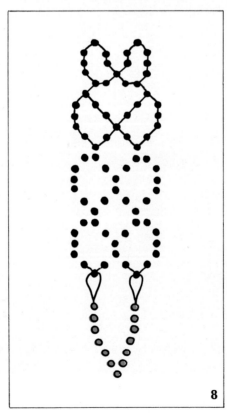

8

WHITE BEAD NECKLACE

Materials

2 packets small white embroidery beads
Linen beading thread
Necklace fastening (jeweller's findings)
2 beading needles

Method

Cut a length of thread 90 ins long. Thread a needle on both ends. Thread 12 beads on to the thread and centre the beads. Pass both needles through one more bead. Thread 6 beads on to the left-hand needle and 6 beads on to the right, then pass both needles through one more bead (see diagram 6). Continue threading the same way until the necklace is the desired length or until most of the thread has been used. Make a loop of 18 beads on one end, taking one end of thread back through the fourth bead and knotting off the thread. Knot a large bead onto the other end of the necklace.

BLACK AND YELLOW NECKLACE

Materials

1 packet yellow beads
1 packet black beads
Linen beading thread or nylon thread
2 beading needles

Method

One whole pattern for the necklace has 12 beads in it, 8 making a complete circle and 4 making a half circle. Thread the first 6 beads of one colour on 90 ins of thread and pass both ends through 2 more beads. Thread 2 more beads of the same colour onto each end of the thread and then cross the ends through 2 beads of the contrast colour. Complete the circle in the second colour with 6 beads, crossing the threads through the last 2 (see diagram 7). Proceed in this way until the necklace is the desired length. Knot off the ends.

CHOKER

Materials

1 packet of small beads in each of the following colours:
    scarlet, black, yellow, white
1 packet mixed small beads
4 beading needles
Linen or nylon thread
1 large bead

Method

The choker is made separately from the single strand attaching ends of the necklace.

Cut two 90 in. lengths of thread and put a needle on both ends of each length. Thread one bead onto each length and pin the beads to a pin cushion or a

Right: *Knitted Golf Club Covers.*

beading board.

Follow the diagram for the pattern (see diagram 8), using the four ends as indicated. The necklace illustrated has 3 repeats in black, 8 in yellow, 3 in black, 8 in scarlet, 3 in black, 8 in yellow, finishing with 3 black. Fasten off the 4 ends by crossing ends and threading back through 3 patterns.

Make the looped end by cutting a 16 in. length of thread and putting a needle on each end. Thread 28 beads of mixed colours onto the thread passing both needles through the last bead to make a loop. Thread single beads onto both threads until strand measures 5 ins. Separate threads. Thread 8 beads onto each. Pass threads through the loops of the last choker pattern (black) and back through the 8 beads. Knot off. This fastens the choker section to the strand. Make the other strand fastening in the same way but begin by threading on a single large bead.

K

KNITTING

Knitting is one of the most popular and practised handicrafts of all.

Striking effects can be achieved in knitting by choosing and mixing colours imaginatively and by using different types of yarn. Try knitting an evening shawl using gold yarn, or some dainty lace edging using cotton. Beads can be actually knitted into a pattern to add a touch of sparkle and glamour.

Knitting patterns always state the type of yarn and the size of needles to be used. Even more important than these, however, is to make sure the tension of your knitting corresponds with that given in the instructions. If it does not, the finished article will be the wrong size. Tension is given in terms of numbers of rows and stitches to 1 in. Test the tension of your knitting before beginning an article, by knitting a square using the yarn and needles quoted in the pattern. Then measure it to see if it is correct. If you find your knitting is too tight or too loose, change to larger or smaller needles to compensate.

GOLF CLUB COVERS

Materials

2 ozs Double Knitting wool (knitting worsted), in each of blue, red, emerald and yellow

1 pair each of Nos. 7 (6), 8 (5) and 9 (4) knitting needles;

Medium sized crochet hook

Tension: 5½ sts and 7 rows to 1 inch.

Measurements: To fit Nos. 4, 3, 2 and 1 clubs approx. 8¾ ins in length.

Abbreviations: See page 5. Also RS = rice stitch.

Method

No. 4 Cover: With blue and No. 8 (5) needles, cast on 50 sts.

** *1st row:* K.2, * p.2, k.2, rep. from * to end.

2nd row: K.2, * p.2, k.2, rep. from * to end. Rep. these 2 rows 5 times more, change to No. 9 (4) needles and cont. until work measures 3 ins from beg. End with 2nd row. Makes holes for cord.

Next row: * K.2, w.r.n., p.2 tog., rep. from * to last 2 sts, k.2. Change to No. 8 (5) needles and beg. with 2nd row, work 3 rows in rib and inc. 1 st. at end of last row. Change to No. 7 (6) needles and rice stitch.

1st row: * K.1 t.b.l., p.1, rep. from * to last st., k.1 t.b.l.

2nd row: K. These 2 rows form rice st. Cont. until piece measures 7½ ins from beg., ending with 2nd row. **

Shape Top: 1st row: K.1, (RS.8, k.2 tog.) 5 times.

2nd row: (k.2 tog. t.b.l., k.7) 5 times, k.1.

3rd row: K.1, (RS.6, k.2 tog.) 5 times.

4th row: (K.2 tog. t.b.l., k.5) 5 times, k.1. Cont. to shape thus until

9th row: K.1, (k.2 tog.) 5 times has been completed. Cut wool and secure rem. sts.

No. 3 cover: Work as for No. 4 but casting on 54 sts red wool, working from ** to **. Shape top by beg.

1st row: (RS.9, k.2 tog.) 5 times. Cont. to shape as for No. 4 cover.

No. 2 cover: Work as for No. 4 casting on 58 sts in emerald. Shape top thus:

1st row: (RS.8, k.2 tog.) 5 times, RS.9.

2nd row: (K.2 tog. t.b.l., k.7) 6 times.

3rd row: (RS.6, k.2 tog.) 6 times.

4th row: (K.2 tog. t.b.l., k.5) 6 times. Finish in same way.

No. 1 cover: As for No. 4 but cast on 62 sts in gold.

Shape top: (RS.8, k.2 tog.) 6 times, RS.3.

2nd row: K.3, (k.2 tog. t.b.l., k.7) 6 times.

3rd row: (RS.6, k.2 tog.) 6 times, RS.3.

4th row: K.3, (k.2 tog. t.b.l., k.5) 6 times.

Below: *Flower Trimmed Spectacle Case.*

Cont. to 8th and 9th row and work
8th row: (K.2 tog. t.b.l., k.1) 7 times.
9th row: (K.2 tog.) 7 times. Finish as before.
Join seams and press. Make crochet cord. Thread through holes in each cover.

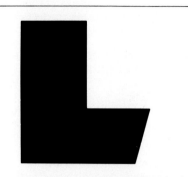

LEATHERWORK

Working with leather can be most rewarding, particularly as leather garments and accessories are so costly to buy. Leather is made from the skin of an animal and is usually bought in a piece the shape of that animal. A complete shape is called a 'skin' and the centre part (i.e. the back of the animal) is usually thicker than at the edges.

Types of leather
Sheepskin: usually the cheapest to buy and often embossed with patterns to make it look like a more expensive type of skin. It can be dyed to a wide range of colours.
Goatskin: sometimes called 'Morocco'. Firmer in texture than sheepskin.
Pigskin: can be distinguished by the grouped markings of 3 little holes (where the bristles grow) found all over it. These are often imitated on other skins, in which case they will be absolutely symmetrical – on real pigskin, the groups vary slightly. It is one of the more expensive leathers.
Calfskin: also rather expensive, but beautifully smooth and supple. The stiffer type of leather that comes from cows is called *Hide* and is generally used for soles of shoes, suitcases and similar items.
Suede: comes from no particular animal, but is soft leather that has been especially treated on the flesh side to give it a 'pile', similar to velvet.
Of these leathers, sheep and goatskins are the easiest to work with as they are the softest. The thickness of leather will vary according to the part of the animal it came from, and also from animal to animal. Do not mix thicknesses in one piece of work – the heavier ones will drag on the lighter ones, weakening, and eventually tearing them. Store all types of leather and suede either flat or rolled up. If several skins are being

rolled up together, they should be interleaved with tissue paper. Suede marks very easily and needs particular care in handling. Roll it with the 'plush' side inside, protected by tissue paper. Never fold any sort of leather, or tie it with string or rubber bands, as it will become permanently marked.

Tools to use on leather
A sharp craft knife or razor-blade should be used to cut leather in order to get clean edges. Blades must be renewed as soon as they get blunt. Never use scissors to cut leather. They will crush the edges

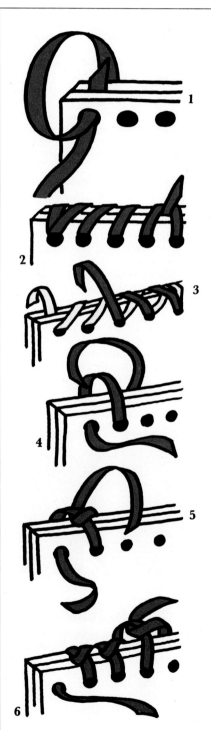

and tear the fibres leaving an uneven and 'fuzzy' line. Leather must be cut on a flat, firm board, which should be discarded when it becomes too scored. Stitch holes should ideally be marked with a stitchmarker, which spaces them evenly. A sharp dressmaker's tracing wheel can be used for this purpose, or if the leather is very thin, stitch holes can be marked by using an unthreaded sewing machine.

Cutting out
Lay the skin out on the board with the right side uppermost so that you can see any flaws which need to be avoided. Place the pattern pieces on top (you will need pattern pieces for every part of the item, including duplications of similar shapes) and draw round each one with a sharp pencil. Do not pin the pattern pieces to the skin as the pins will leave permanent marks. Cut out the shapes, keeping the blade at right angles to the leather to avoid 'undercutting'.
When cutting out items in suede, cut them so the pile lies in one direction only, as with velvet.

Joining leather
As leather cannot be pinned or tacked, the edges can be held together during stitching with spring type clothes pins or bulldog clips, that do not have too fierce a spring. Sticky tape can be used on suede, but it would tear the face of smooth leathers.
Sewing by machine: Set the stitches to a medium size and slacken off the tension a little. Too large a stitch will look unsightly – small ones may tear the leather. If it is difficult to feed the leather smoothly under the foot of the machine, place a layer of tissue paper each side of the skin, stitch through it and tear it away afterwards. Tissue paper placed between the right sides of suede during stitching will protect the pile.
If seams cross each other, trim away the surplus from the first seam before stitching the second. This prevents the extra thickness from getting jammed under the foot of the machine.
In some cases leather can be stuck instead of stitched. Use a rubber-based adhesive as this will not make the leather stiff and hard. Apply it sparingly to both surfaces and wipe away any surplus immediately. Take care nothing gets on the glued surfaces as it will show through when the two pieces are glued together.
Stitching: Use pure silk thread for thin leathers and strong linen thread for the heavier types. If sewing by hand, wax the thread first with candle or beeswax to help it slide more easily through the leather. Mark the stitch holes, then use a saddlemaker's needle to stitch a straight line of running stitches. Stitch back along the same line taking stitches through the holes in the opposite way so you have a

continuous line of stitches on both sides.

Saddle stitching: usually worked in a light coloured thread to contrast with the leather. Use heavy waxed linen thread and 2 needles. Push one needle in from the front to the back and the other from the back to the front, then pull both threads taut. Push the first needle back through to the front and the second through from the front to the back (through the same holes) and pull the threads taut again. Continue in this way. The finished effect will be a neat line of running stitches along both sides of the seam. Do not join the thread in the middle of a seam, unless it is unavoidable. If the leather is thick or coarse, stitching can be facilitated by punching very small holes in the leather with an awl beforehand.

Lacing: an elaborate way of joining pieces of leather, mostly used for the sides of wallets, writing cases, purses and book covers. There are different types of lacing but the basic principle is the same for each. First make holes in the leather, evenly spaced and fairly near the edge. Use either a lacing chisel which makes slits, or a punch, preferably the type which makes one hole while it marks the next, thus ensuring they are equidistant. Laces can be bought ready-cut, or you can cut your own. They should be long enough to work the length of the seam. If you have to join them in the middle, carefully pare away the edges of both pieces to make them thin and wedge-like and stick the ends together overlapping them by about $\frac{1}{4}$ in. Leave to dry completely before using. To make lacing easier, trim the ends of the laces to a diagonal point before starting.

Lacing by spiral stitch: (see diagrams 1 and 2, page 71). Run a single lace through the holes, in a spiral. To hide the ends of the lace, make the first and last loop a double one as shown.

Lacing by cross stitch: (see diagram 3). Lace once along the seam with spiral stitch, then bring another lace back through the same holes but in the opposite direction.

Lacing by buttonhole stitch: (see diagrams 4, 5 and 6). Thread the lace through the holes to make a loop, then pass the ends of the lace under the loop as shown. Pull tight to make a decorative 'knot'.

Pressing leather

Leather should be pressed with a warm dry iron (not steam), applied over a press cloth or thick pad of brown paper. Press down fairly firmly, but do not rub the iron up and down on the skin.

FLOWER-TRIMMED SPECTACLE CASE

Materials

2 pieces red suede, at least 8 × 4$\frac{1}{2}$ ins
Fabric for lining to tone with suede
Scraps of yellow and blue suede
Matching red, yellow and blue silk sewing thread
Rubber based adhesive
Gilt spectacle case frame, 3$\frac{1}{4}$ ins wide

Method

Transfer the pattern on page 70, enlarging it accordingly (1 square = 1 in.). Use it as a template to cut 2 shapes from the lining fabric. Trim off the top part of the template along the dotted line and use the pattern again, minus this hem allowance, to cut 2 shapes from red suede.

Cut out the 2 flower motifs from yellow suede, and 2 circles (use a small coin as template) from the blue suede. Centre the blue circles onto the yellow flower shapes and stick in place with the adhesive. When thoroughly dry, stitch round the edge of the circles with blue silk.

Position the flower shapes on the main red shapes and glue in place. When dry, stitch round the edge with the yellow silk thread.

Place the red shapes together, with the *right* sides inside and stitch along the sides and base, from notch to notch. Turn right side out. Stitch lining together from notch to notch in the same way. Trim seam to $\frac{1}{4}$ in. with pinking shears, then turn top hem allowance over to the *wrong* side and tack in place. Fit lining inside case and slipstitch top edges together from notch to notch.

Spread a little adhesive around the inside of the frame and press case top into this carefully. Leave to dry thoroughly. When adhesive is dry, stitch carefully in place through the holes in frame, using running stitches in double red silk.

MACHINE EMBROIDERY

Many sewing machines are equipped with gadgets that make it possible to work all kinds of embroidery stitches straight onto the fabric. However, the ordinary straight stitch that all sewing machines produce can be used most effectively in embroidery designs. To work embroidery in this way, the presser foot is removed to allow greater freedom of movement. Mount a piece of material in a circular embroidery frame and practice machining straight and curved lines and circles to get the feel of using a machine in this way.

MACHINE-EMBROIDERED WASTEPAPER BIN

Materials

A tin, 7$\frac{1}{4}$ ins tall and 5$\frac{1}{2}$ ins diameter
Blue linen-type fabric 8$\frac{1}{4}$ × 19 ins
Scraps of felt in light, medium and dark pink
8 large pink wooden beads
1 skein six stranded thread in following colours: lilac, mauve-pink, medium dusty pink and deep pink
Reels (balls) of thread in black, pale and dark pink and blue to match the material

Method

To enlarge the diagram on page 74, cut a piece of paper 8 ins square and divide into 1 in. squares. Copy the design on to this (see page 42).

Trace the design on to tracing paper and place it on the right side of the material, 1$\frac{3}{4}$ ins away from one side and $\frac{1}{2}$ in. away from the top and bottom edges, with a piece of carbon paper face down on the material under the tracing paper. Draw over the lines, keeping the tracing paper firmly in position so that the design is transferred to the fabric. Repeat the process 1$\frac{1}{4}$ in. away from the other side of the fabric reversing the tracing paper so that the design is transferred the other way round.

Remove the presser foot from the machine and lower the 'drop feed'. Mount the fabric in a 7-ins diameter embroidery frame so that the first design to be worked is held tightly in the centre. Using the tracing as a pattern, cut out the felt in 3 shades of pink as shown on the diagram and machine stitch in place with pale pink cotton. Thread the machine with dark pink cotton and place the embroidery ring under the needle. Work 3 rows of stitching along the 4 upright lines of the design and then, moving the ring backwards and forwards, fill in the top 2 circles on the left hand side and the bottom 3 circles on the right hand side.

Thread the machine with pale pink cotton, and work 1 line of stitching near each of the 3 pink ones you have just worked. Then machine once over the lower lines of the design. Fill in the rest of the circles.

Thread the machine with black cotton and work a line of stitching next to each of the pale pink lines and another line next to – but not quite as long as – each

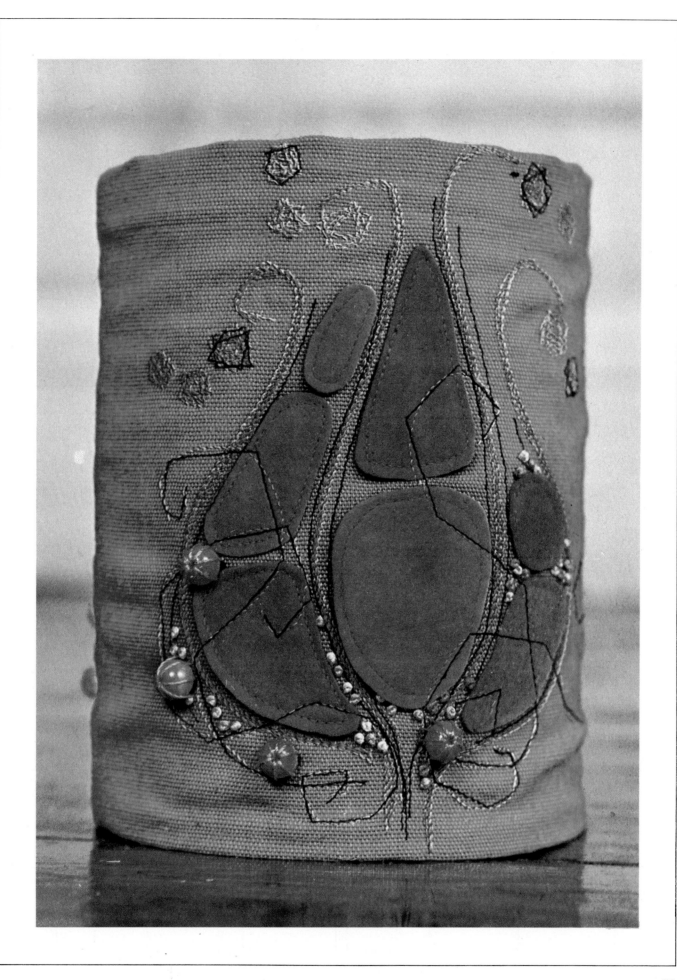

of the four upright lines (see illustration). Finish off the black stitching by machine stitching a single line around one of each of the 4 groups of circles.

Repeat these embroidery instructions for the pattern on the other side, working the top 2 circles on the right hand side and the bottom 3 on the left hand side in dark pink cotton and the rest in pale pink cotton.

Stitch the beads in place as indicated with stranded cotton, using 3 strands and taking 6 or 8 stitches through the centre of each bead. Finish off the embroidery by working clusters of French knots in the 2 shades of pink stranded cotton using 6 strands (see instructions right). Repeat this for the other design as well and, with the right sides together, machine stitch along the shorter edge taking a ½-in. seam allowance. Turn a single ½-in. hem to the wrong side along the top and bottom edges and herringbone in position (see page 18). Turn the fabric the right way out and put over tin.

Below: *Pattern Diagram for Wastepaper Bin.*

Key
A *Pale Pink Felt*
B *Medium Pink Felt*
C *Dark Pink Felt*
• *Clusters of French Knots*
⊕ *Pink Wooden Beads*
French knots: Bring the needle through

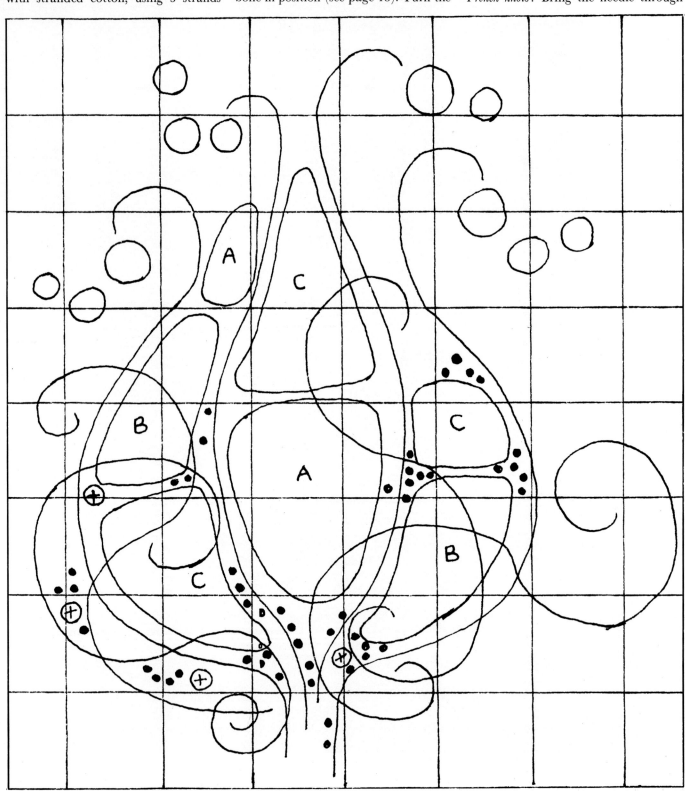

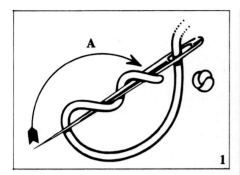

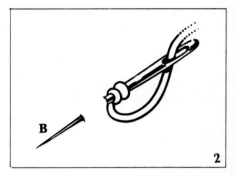

from the back. Hold a short length of yarn in position with the thumb and twist the needle under the yarn (A) (see diagram 1), 2 or 3 times. Return the needle to the point next to where it came out and pull through, holding the yarn taut (B) (see diagram 2).

MOBILES

Making mobiles has practically become a handicraft in its own right! So popular have mobiles become over the last few years that the scope for making them has widened considerably, as more and more people have used their imaginations to good effect. They may be made from all kinds of materials – blocks of wood, plastic shapes, scraps of fabric and wool, and all kinds of paper and card, to name just some. They may be suspended from circular frames, lengths of wire or strips of wood – the more complicated ones presenting something of a challenge if they are to balance correctly. Although mainly thought of as nursery decorations, more sophisticated mobiles, in balance and design, look extremely effective hung elsewhere in the house.

PIXIE RING MOBILE

Materials
5 table tennis balls
Felt squares in bright colours
Flesh-coloured poster paint
Flesh-coloured felt
Black poster paint, ink or small adhesive labels
Pipe cleaners
Brown double knitting wool (knitting worsted), about 4 yds

Large and small coloured beads
9 in. diameter lampshade ring
1 small brass curtain ring
$\frac{7}{8}$ yd braid trimming
Black sewing thread
Black button thread
Fabric adhesive
Clear all-purpose adhesive

Method

Trace off and cut out separate paper patterns for one hand, the jerkin and the trousers from the outlines shown below. Follow the broken lines for the hand and trousers. Cut a 3 in. diameter half-circle for the hat.

Cut the hand shape out twice in flesh coloured felt and the jerkin and trousers twice each in gay coloured felt. Cut out the hat shape once in a felt to match either the jerkin or the trousers.

Stitch 2 small coloured beads down the centre of one jerkin piece for front buttons. Place the back jerkin piece flat and stick a hand at each end of the sleeve as shown in the diagram. Stick

one trouser piece to the jerkin back putting adhesive on the upper part only and positioning as shown.

Cut a piece of pipe cleaner 4 ins long and bend it into the shape of the coloured line in the diagram. Stick it into position. Stick the second trouser piece over the first and finally the front of the jerkin on top. Spread adhesive sparingly all over sleeves, across top and down each side. To make the head, pierce a small hole in a table tennis ball with a thick needle and then paint the ball flesh-coloured. When the paint is dry, push the ball down over the protruding pipe cleaner. To make the hair, cut a piece of cardboard about 4 ins deep and wind the brown wool (yarn) round it about 15 times. Slide the loops off the cardboard and tie tightly in the middle. Cut the ends and spread out the wool (yarn) into a circle. Stick this to the ball, the tied centre at the crown and trim the ends neatly. Paint in the eyes. Form the hat into a cone and stick the straight edges together. Smear a little adhesive round

the brim of the hat and stick the hat onto the hair. Make four more pixies in the same way. To make up the mobile, knot the end of a piece of black sewing thread and catch it firmly to the top of a hat. Slide a large bead to rest on top of the hat and then tie the other end of the thread to the lampshade ring, about 6 ins above the figure. Fix the remaining pixies around the circle in the same way. Cut 4 15-in. lengths of black button thread. Loop each one through the curtain ring and knot about $1\frac{1}{2}$ ins above the cut ends of each pair. Then tie each doubled thread at quarterly intervals round the ring. Glue braid round the ring to finish off.

MONOGRAMS

Embroidering decorative letters on to household articles and clothes can add an attractive personal touch.

Any style of letter may be used, and there is a variety of stitches suitable for working the letter. If two letters are arranged so one is interwoven with the other this is known as a cipher; when the letters share the same upright stroke – so neither is quite complete in itself – this is a monogram. The style of lettering chosen should obviously be in keeping with the item it is to decorate – sheets, pillowcase and guest towels, for example, which provide a plain linen base can take fairly ornate letters, but if letters are to be embroidered on to a modern blouse or fashion accessory then a plainer type may be more appropriate.

Experiment with lettering on squared paper to find styles that appeal to you. Look through newspapers and magazines at headings and if you see letters which you think could be adapted to give a basis for embroidery, trace them off and transfer to squared paper. This allows you accurately to assess the measurements of each letter and to find ways in which they harmonize with each other.

Stitches

Any type of stitch may be used to work lettering, but the simpler stitches are usually the most effective. Cross stitch (see page 39), for instance, looks pleasing when used to work a fairly plain style of letter. Other stitches which work well are chain stitch, and stem stitch (see pages 18 and 34). Satin stitch, (see page 34), however is probably the most popular and widely used stitch for lettering and can be used on its own, or combined with other stitches.

Padded satin stitch: This gives a rich appearance to embroidery and is particularly suitable for the more ornate style of letter. Work an outline round the

Right: *Embroidered Tunic Motif.*

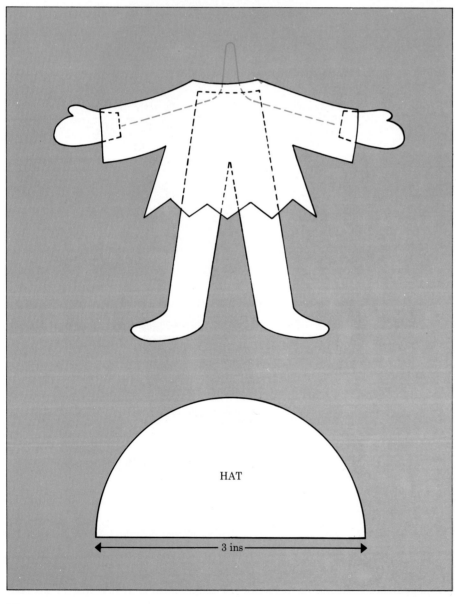

HAT

←——— 3 ins ———→

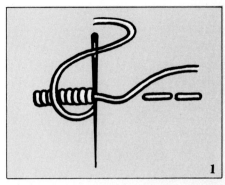

letter first with chain (see page 18), or running stitches, then fill in the areas between the outline lines with chain stitches until every part of the letter is covered. Finally work satin stitches over the padding of chain stitches, keeping stitches close together, very regular and all slanting in the same direction.

Cording: This technique is suitable for small, fairly plain letters. Lay a thread along the line of the letter (this is the cording thread), then with another thread, known as the top or working thread, work vertical stitches close together over the cording thread until it is completely covered (see diagram 1). Cording looks most effective when it is worked in a thick, well-twisted thread.

TUNIC MOTIF

Materials
Plain-coloured tunic top with long ties
Stranded cotton in suitable colour
No. 6 crewel needle

Method

Make full size diagrams of the applicable letters from the chart (left – 1 square = 1 in.). Trace the letters onto a tie of the tunic in an attractive group. (If you wish to combine letters into a cipher or a monogram, experiment on a piece of paper to find the best linking arrangement of the letters, *before* tracing onto the tunic tie.)

Work each letter in satin stitch or padded satin stitch using 3 strands of embroidery cotton throughout. Press the embroidery lightly on the wrong side.

NORWEAVE EMBROIDERY

Norweave embroidery, which as its name suggests originated in Norway, is especially recommended for beginners in canvas work, or for those in a hurry, as it produces fairly quick results. It consists of blocks of satin stitch worked over 3 horizontal and vertical double threads of canvas. It can be used for pictures, panels, cushions or anywhere where a bold design is suitable.

NORWEAVE BELT

Materials

$3\frac{1}{2} \times 28$ ins piece of double thread canvas, 10 threads to 1 in.

2 skeins each Tapestry Wool in dark, medium and light colours

3×28 ins piece of lining material

Matching thread for lining

3 press studs

Note The length of the belt can be adjusted by approx $1\frac{3}{4}$ ins which is the measurement of one pattern repeat (18 stitches).

Method

Start working the design from the chart (see diagram 1) leaving 4 double threads unworked at each edge for turning in. Work in satin stitch (see page 34) taken over 3 double threads each way. Try not to catch your wool on the raw edges of the canvas or it will fray and weaken.

To make up: Press the completed embroidery lightly, with a damp cloth

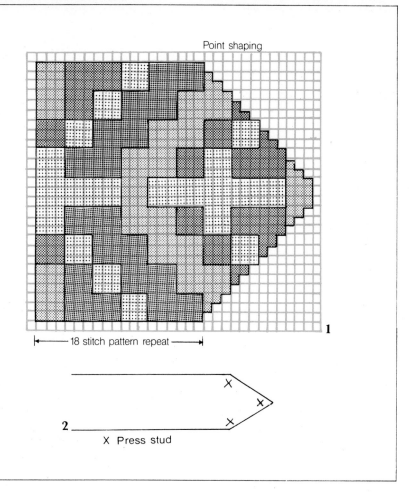

Point shaping

|← 18 stitch pattern repeat →| **1**

X Press stud   **2**

and warm iron. Fold over turnings to wrong side of work and baste, neatening the point. Baste hems on lining to correspond and handstitch lining in position on wrong side of embroidery with slip stitches. Sew press studs as indicated (see diagram 2), making sure that the pattern matches when belt is fastened.

NURSERY ACCESSORIES

Nursery accessories are usually expensive to buy, and yet extremely necessary. Many of them, however, can be made, quickly and enjoyably at home, thus cutting costs to a minimum. In addition, you can plan them in colours and fabrics that blend with the décor of the nursery. The changing mattress and wall tidy patterns given here will be invaluable assets for young mothers. The laminated surface of the mattress makes it easy to keep clean and the raised sides help to protect a young baby from draughts when he is being washed or changed. The wall tidy has been designed with an assortment of pockets to hold all the 'baby paraphernalia'. It would be equally as acceptable in an older child's room, however, to hold pencils, rulers etc.

CHANGING MATTRESS

Materials
1¾ yds laminated fabric or PVC
Matching thread
1 in. thick sheet of foam – 15 × 24 ins
2 bags foam filling
Adhesive tape
Felt tipped pen
(Size when completed – 33 × 14 ins)

Method
Make a paper pattern for the mattress, by enlarging the shape shown in diagram 1, (see page 42 – 5 squares = 1 in.) and use it to cut out 2 pieces of fabric for the top and underside.
Place pieces of fabric together with right sides facing each other. Instead of pinning, bind together at intervals with strips of adhesive tape. Machine round edge, leaving a ½ in. seam allowance. Leave the base open and also a 3 in. gap for filling at the top end. Clip seam allowance on corners and turn mattress the right way out.
Place the foam sheet inside the mattress. With felt-tipped pen mark out the inner sewing line, (dotted line on diagram 1), ½ in. from the edge of foam. Pin carefully in 3 places along sewing line on each side. Remove the foam.
The shiny side of PVC fabric sticks to the machine when it is sewn. To avoid this tape strips of paper over sewing line on both sides of mattress. Mark out the

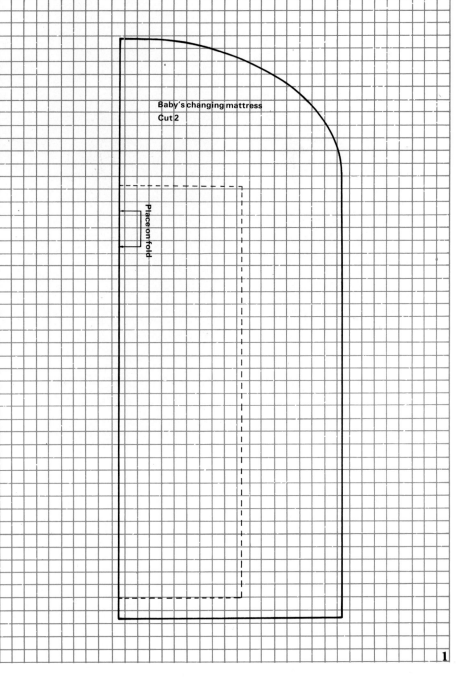

Baby's changing mattress
Cut 2

Place on fold

1

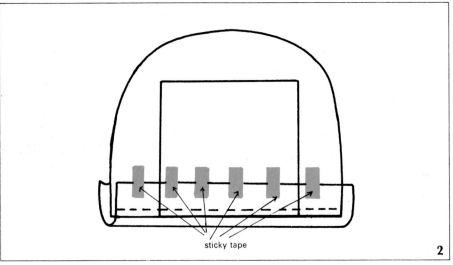

sticky tape

2

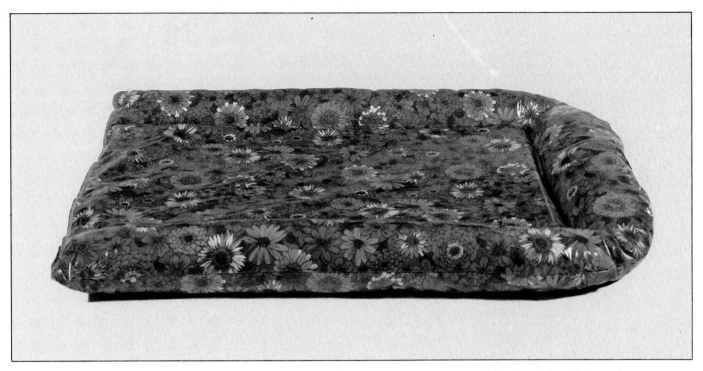

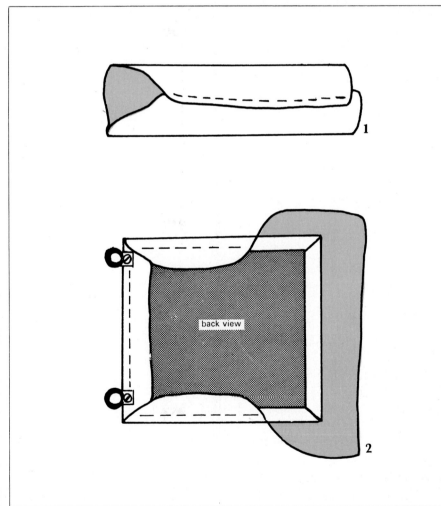

mattress to cover sewing line. If necessary, mark sewing line with a pen. Finish off base with row of zigzag stitch. Remove paper and adhesive tape. Cut away remaining fabric below sewing line (see diagram 2, opposite page).

WALL TIDY

Materials
Piece of hardboard 22 × 28 ins with ½ in. battens pinned around edges to make a frame (see diagram 2)
1¼ yds PVC coated fabric or other strong material
18 in. length of tape
Scraps of fabric for appliqué (optional)
Adhesive tape
2 metal hangers (see diagram 2)
Felt tipped pen

Method
Using the top part of the chart on page 82 make paper patterns of the pockets (see page 42 – 1 square = 1 inch). Then cut out a piece of fabric for the backing 40 × 34 ins (see bottom part of chart). Also cut out all the pockets from the fabric. Fold the raw edges of the tops of the pockets under and keep in place with strips of adhesive tape. Fold strips of pattern paper over the area to be sewn and keep in place with strips of adhesive tape, to avoid the fabric sticking when it is machined. Machine pocket tops. Remove paper and tape.
Make a complete paper pattern of the finished tidy from the lower part of the chart. Cut out the pocket shapes from this and then lay the paper pattern (with cut outs) over the backing fabric. Mark the position of each pocket onto the backing fabric with faint pinpricks or felt tipped pen (which wipes off).

sewing line on the paper also and remove pins. Machine carefully, leaving the base open. Remove paper and tape.
Slide the foam sheet into place. Fill sides tightly with foam chips, using a rolling pin to help push filling into place. Fill top and neaten off seam with oversewing.
Secure the base with strips of adhesive tape, so the top side is fixed to the underside. Place paper on both sides of the

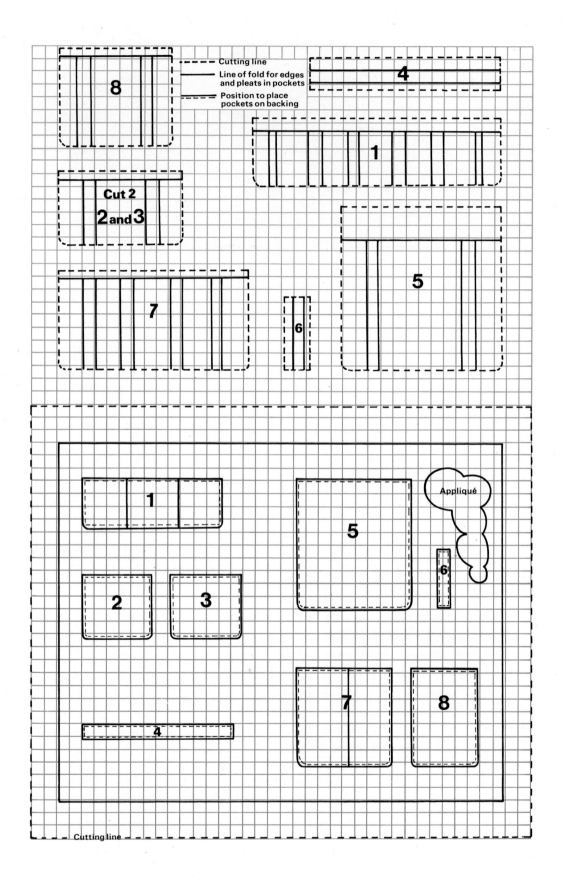

Make neat knife pleats on both sides of each pocket (see markings on top part of chart). Secure pockets into position with adhesive tape. Tape the paper pattern pocket shapes cut out from the complete wall tidy pattern over each pocket to make the PVC easy to sew. Machine in place. Remove paper and sticky tape. Complete one pocket before moving on to next and if the fabric shows signs of fraying, sew round the edges of the pockets with zigzag stitch.

Fold the paper roll holder (No. 4 on chart) in 3, lengthways. Secure with tape and machine along centre to hold edges (see diagram 1, page 81). Fold under the ends and machine. Machine one end on to the backing fabric. Attach 9 ins of the tape to the other end, and a further 9 ins to the backing, so the holder can be undone easily when a new paper roll is needed.

Deal with safety-pin holder (No. 6 in the chart) in the same way, machining it on to the backing at each end. Make slots to hold pins with short rows of stitching at half-inch intervals.

Tape and stitch appliqué into position under the paper pattern.

Pull holdall tightly over the hardboard square and staple tightly into position on the wood at the back (see diagram 2, page 81). Attach 2 metal hangers either side at the top for fixing tidy to the wall.

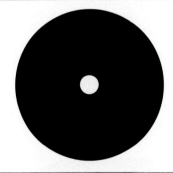

ORIGAMI

Origami is a highly specialized art of paper folding. It originated in China centuries ago and was later introduced into Japan. Indeed it is the Japanese who have developed the technique.

True origami is effected by *only* folding regularly-shaped sheets of paper – that is to say it involves *no* cutting or pasting once the work has begun. Many modern origami patterns bend these rules!

DISPLAY COLLAR

Materials
Thin card
Gold-covered foil
Wallpaper paste
Pinking shears and scissors

83

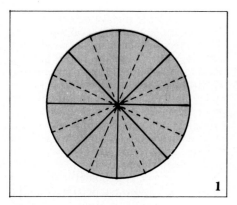

1

Method

Cut a 5 in. diameter circle in card and cover with the foil. Then draw a 3½ in. diameter in the centre and mark the outer circle into eight equal sections. Cut away the centre circle and trim the outer edge with pinking shears.

Cut two circles of foil paper, twice as large as the original circle (10 in. diameter) and stick them back-to-back with the wallpaper paste. Pink the edge with shears as before. Draw a 6 in. diameter circle in the centre and fold in half exactly across the centre and crease sharply. Open out and fold across the centre again so the folds form a cross exactly at right angles. Open out and fold a third and fourth time, exactly between previous folds. Turn paper over and repeat again, these folds falling exactly between the first set (see diagram 1). Open out paper and cut away centre circle, then re-fold outer edge in a star shape and cut a ¾ in. slit in each outer fold, ½ in. above the lower edge. Carefully fit the card circle round the star and slot into the cuts, each point of the star falling at a marked point on the rim. Secure with a pin pushed up through the rim inside the fold of each point.

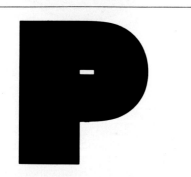

PAPERWORK

Paper has tremendous potential as a craft material. The wide variety of different papers available, in assorted colours, textures, designs and weights gives amazing scope for making all manner of things. In general, its cheapness and disposability means you can make something to suit particular circumstances without the thought of living with it for ever, or if you make a mistake, you can start again without incurring massive costs. Basic materials for paperwork are a pair of scissors, a sharp cutting knife, pencils, ruler and perhaps paints or coloured pens or pencils. All-purpose adhesives, wallpaper paste, or any clear or white glue are suitable for sticking paper.

ALL-THE-YEAR ASTERS

Materials

Crepe paper in bright green and deep leaf green for leaves and yellow, pink, and mauve etc., for petals
Florists' wire
18 in. long thin garden stakes
Cotton wool
Fine wire or thread
Adhesive tape
Fabric adhesive

Method

Hook over the tip of a length of florists' wire and wrap a scrap of cotton wool round it, moulding it into a firm ball a little bigger than a large pea. Cut a 3-in. diameter circle of bright green crepe paper, place it centrally over the cotton wool, bring the edges down all round, and secure tightly with fine wire or thread (see diagram 1).

Cut 2 9-in long strips, 3 ins wide, in yellow crepe with grain running widthways (see diagram 2). Fold each in half lengthways, as indicated by the broken line. Cut a closely spaced ¼-in. deep fringe, along the folded edge of each piece, open out, turn over, and re-fold along the line of the previous fold – but do not crease. Stick the two strips together along the lower edge, then wind the double strip round and round the green centre – the cut edges level with it – sticking along the base at intervals to hold in place.

Cut 2 12-in. long strips, 3 ins wide, for the petals, the grain running as shown by the arrow (see diagram 3). Cut each piece down to within ½ in. of the lower edge all the way along to form a fringe.

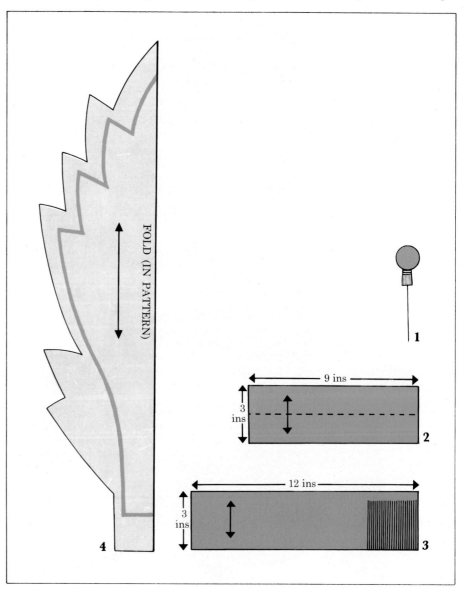

Stick strips together along the lower edge, as before. Wind this double strip round the centre, keeping absolutely level and sticking the lower edge of the petals ½ in. above the lower edge of the yellow strips. Fix a garden stake to the wire with adhesive tape, for the stem.

Trace the large and small leaf patterns, (see diagram 4), following the outer and inner lines respectively. Cut 2 large and 3 small shapes in leaf green (grain running as indicated by the arrow). Cut an 18-in. long strip, ½ in. wide in green crepe with the grain running across. Stick one end round the base of the petals, wind round once, and then bind in the bases of the three small leaves evenly round the flower, securing with a little adhesive. Continue to wrap the strip round the base of the flower, then slowly twist it round and down the stem – binding in the two large leaves as you go. Secure the end of the strip with tape.

Open out the petals and curl gently, but firmly, stroking them between the ball of your thumb and the blade of your scissors. Curl the leaves in the same way.

PATCHWORK

Patchwork is one of the oldest crafts in the world, dating back, in some crude forms, to centuries before the birth of Christ. It probably has its roots in necessity, when patches of fabrics were saved to be joined together to create a new whole, or to repair worn garments. The decorative aspects emerged some time later, and many of the beautiful, and now traditional, patchwork patterns were originated by the early American settler women, who used them mainly in the construction of bed-quilts.

In its original form, there was little attempt at any pattern in patchwork. The arrangement was governed only by the size of the fragments that were stitched together. As the decorative aspect was realized, so in most cases, these patches evolved into regular geometric shapes, which began to be organised into clearly defined patterns. Nowadays, most, although not all, patchwork, involves the use of geometric shapes, of which hexagons are probably the favourites. Others that are commonly used are squares (the easiest of all to work), triangles and diamonds. Additional shapes are illustrated right.

One of the most important aspects of patchwork is the mixing of colours and many of the magnificent designs rely very heavily on the subtle and clever placing of colour to realize their full effect.

Patchwork Shapes and Patterns
Commonly used patchwork shapes include hexagons, squares, triangles, dia-monds and pentagons. These can be used on their own with fabrics of random colours, or with planned colour placings to form various designs. Alternatively they can be used in conjunction with one another to form more specialised designs, in which case, the colour combinations are more important.

Squares and triangles. Illustrated opposite are some suggested ways of combining these shapes to make patterns. Each of these could be used as a single block in a piece of patchwork – perhaps to make a cushion, bedspread, table-cloth, etc. To save time, if you are making a large item, they would all look effective if interspersed with plain blocks of equal size in a colour that blends with that of the patchwork.

Hexagons. These can be combined together in rosettes, in diamond shapes (see diagram 1, page 88) or in stripes (diagrams 2, 3 and 4), but all these effects rely on clever colour positioning of the different patches. They can also be used to make attractive borders (see diagram 5). Hexagons can be of any size, but ideally they should be between 1 in. (each side) to 3 in.

Diamonds. Diamond shapes are useful and effective in making star patterns, and the diagrams on opposite page show them used in six and eight-point stars. The eight-point star has been finished off with square and triangular shapes to make a complete square block. Extra care should be taken when cutting diamond shapes to ensure they are accurate, as they are the most difficult of all geometric shapes to fit together.

The diagram below the star patterns shows diamonds arranged in a traditional pattern called 'Tumbling Blocks'. It is most effective when carried out in diamonds of three shades, of which one should be dark.

Other Shapes. Illustrated right are some other shapes that can be used in patchwork patterns. They can be combined most effectively with the shapes already discussed, in a variety of ways.

How to do Patchwork
The following instructions explain how to cut out and join pentagon shapes together in patchwork. Because of their shape, pentagons used on their own always combine into a 'ball' formation, but next to the square, they are the easiest shape to work with, as their wide angles make for ease of joining. The principles of cutting and joining patchwork shapes are the same whatever shape you are using, and whether the finished work is to be flat or 'ball-shaped'.

In any patchwork using geometric shapes, you must first make templates to ensure all patches are exactly the same. Either trace off the pentagon shape illustrated on page 90, or for great-

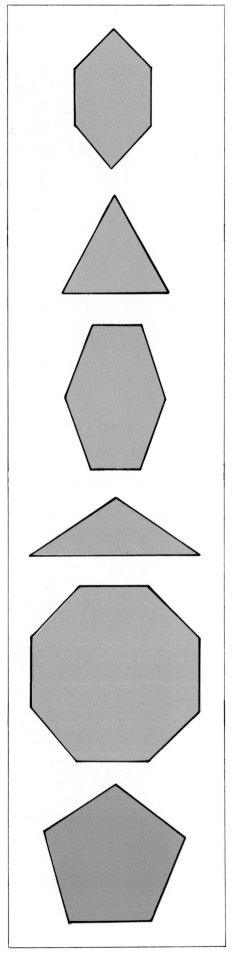

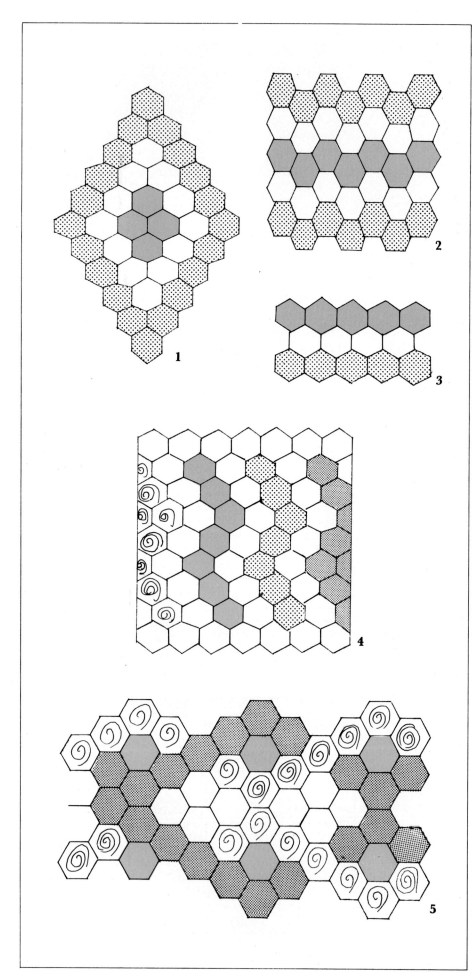

1

2

3

4

5

er accuracy, draw your own. The more accurate the template, the better the finished patchwork will be. Two templates are required for patchwork – one is used for cutting out the fabric pieces and the other – to cut out the backing papers.

To draw a pentagon template with $1\frac{1}{2}$ in. sides, on stiff card, draw a horizontal line exactly $1\frac{1}{2}$ ins long. Place a protractor so that the 90 degrees line is exactly on the left end of the line and mark with a pencil dot the angle of 72 degrees (see diagram 1, page 90). Join the dot and the left side of the horizontal line and make this line exactly $1\frac{1}{2}$ ins long. Turn the card and place the 90 degrees line of the protractor on the end of the line and again mark 72 degrees. Continue, always working on the left side of the line and drawing to the left, making the line $1\frac{1}{2}$ ins long each time. When all the lines are joined together in an enclosed shape, you will have drawn a pentagon, (see diagram 2, page 90). Cut out the completed shape very carefully with a very sharp pointed knife and using a metal edged rule.

If this template is to be the one used to cut out the fabric pieces, you will need to draw and cut out another pentagon shape on stiff card in exactly the same way, but making the sides only 1 in. long. This will then be used to cut out the backing papers.

Cutting out fabrics and backing papers: Press all the creases out of the fabrics you are going to use and lay them on a flat surface. Place the template on the wrong side of the fabric and draw round the shape with a sharply pointed soft pencil. Cut out as many shapes as you require. Always use the same type of fabric throughout any one piece of patchwork. If different kinds of fabric are used, the seams are liable to break open.

Using the smaller (i.e. backing) template, draw and cut out the same number of paper shapes as fabric patches. They must be very accurately cut or the patchwork will not lie flat.

Making and joining patches: Pin a backing paper to the centre, wrong side of a fabric shape (see diagram 3, page 90). Fold the turnings to the wrong side and baste to the backing paper (see diagrams 4 and 5). When all the backing papers have been basted to the fabric shapes, place 2 patches together, right sides facing, and oversew together using tiny stitches (see diagram 6). Do not tie a knot at the end of the thread – lay the end along the tops of the patches and oversew over it. Push the needle through the fabric only, (not the backing paper) at right angles to the edge so that the stitches are neat. To fasten off, work back about 4 stitches. Several patches

Right: *Patchwork Pram Cover*

can be joined together without breaking the thread, but always strengthen the corners with 2 or 3 stitches.
The finishing off will vary according to the patchwork.
Finishing off a ball made from pentagon shapes is explained under the **Method** for the Perfume Ball below. Many patchwork items, however, will involve the technique used for finishing off 'flat patchwork'. This is done as follows.
When all the patches are joined, press them on the wrong side with a warm iron, keeping the backing papers in position. Take out the paper shapes and baste all round the edge of the work to keep the turnings of the edge patches secure. Press again to remove any marks made by the basting. Mount on to lining or on to the main article with slip stitches. Catch down large areas of patchwork to the lining at regular points.

PERFUME BALL

Materials

Scraps of cotton or silk fabric in toning colours and matching patterns
Matching thread
Stiff paper for backing
Stiff card for templates
Loose lavender or potpourri
2 yards satin baby ribbon

Method

Make fabric and backing pentagon-shaped templates with $1\frac{1}{2}$-in. and 1-in. sides from stiff card. Cut out 12 backing templates using the smaller shape and 12 shapes in assorted colours of fabric using the larger shape. Baste the fabric pieces to the backing templates, and then stitch 11 of them together in a ball shape as previously described. Fill the ball with lavender packed quite tightly and then stitch the remaining 3 sides of the last patch. Just before taking the last stitches, fold and stitch a cluster of ribbon loops and push the ends into the ball. Stitch off the last patch, securing the ribbon ends. Make a 6 inch hanging loop and stitch this into the middle of the cluster of ribbon loops.

Stitches

Fly stitch: Bring the needle out on the right side of fabric at A, (see diagram 1, page 92). Insert it to right of A and bring it through again at B. Make a small back-

Right: *Pattern for Patchwork Pram Cover*
Stitch and Colour Key
— *dark emerald, feather stitch*
↞ *wedgewood blue, single row of fly stitch*
⋙ *medium dark blue, double row of fly stitch, dark blue on outside and pale blue on inside*
--- *dark emerald, backstitch*
-ooo- *backstitch threaded with bright canary yellow and wine-mauve*
● *medium dark blue, French knots*

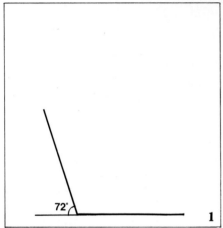

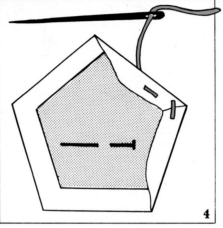

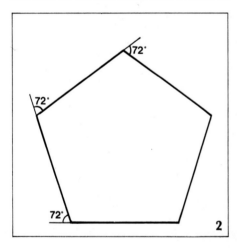

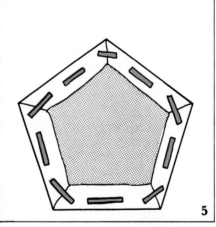

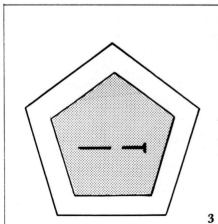

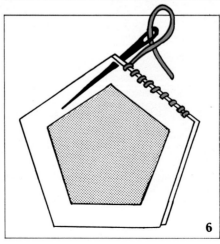

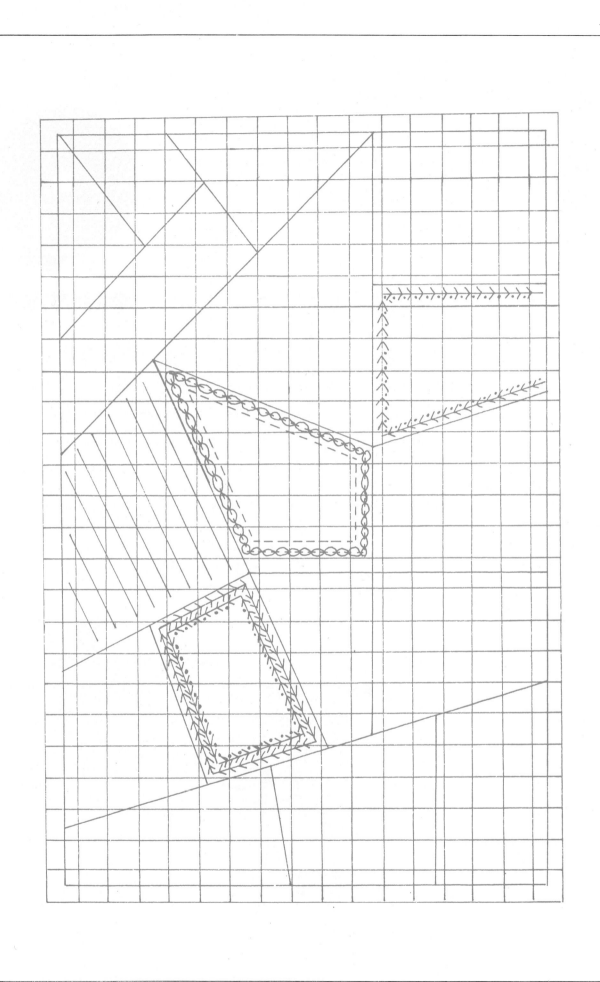

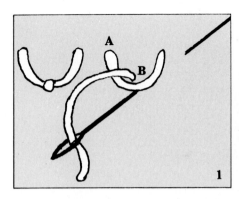

medium dark blue, emerald, bright canary yellow and wine-mauve
One sheet of thin card

Method

Rule a piece of paper 17× 25 ins into 1 in. squares and copy the diagram (see page 91). Trace the shapes on to the thin card and cut them out. Place these card templates on to the wrong side of the scraps of fabric and cut out the shapes, allowing $\frac{1}{4}$ in. extra all the way round for turnings.

Tack the fabric pieces to the card along the edges, the right side of the material facing upwards. Do this with all the pieces of material and then oversew [overcast] them together along the edges.

Remove the pieces of card and, following the stitch and colour key work French knots, feather stitch, (see pages 74 and 78), fly stitch, backstitch and threaded backstitch (see left), in the positions indicated.

Cut 5 $3\frac{1}{2}$-in. wide strips on the cross from the mauve cotton and sew them all together. Machine stitch a $\frac{1}{2}$ in. hem along 1 edge and gather the other, $\frac{1}{2}$ in. away from the edge.

Cut a rectangle of pink lining material 24× 17 ins and a rectangle of wadding 23× 16 ins. Turn $\frac{1}{2}$ in. under all the way round the edge of the patchwork, draw up the frill to fit around the edge and tack in place, with the right side of the frill to the wrong side of the patchwork. Lay the piece of wadding on the wrong side of the patchwork and tack in place. Turn in $\frac{1}{2}$ in. along the edges of the lining material. Tack it to wrong side of patchwork on top of wadding along the edges.

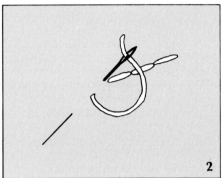

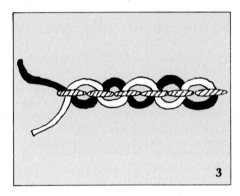

stitch to anchor the stitch in place. This stitch can be worked singly or in a vertical line.

Backstitch: Bring the needle through the right side of the fabric and make a small backward stitch. Bring the needle through the fabric again, the same distance in front of the first stitch as the first stitch is long. Insert the needle at the point where it first came through, (see diagram 2).

Threaded backstitch: Work a foundation [initial] row of backstitch and thread up and down with different coloured threads working one colour one way and one the other, (see diagram 3).

EMBROIDERED PATCHWORK PRAM COVER

Materials

$\frac{1}{2}$ yd of 36 ins wide pink lining material
$\frac{1}{2}$ yd of 36 ins wide mauve cotton lawn
$\frac{1}{2}$ yd of 36 ins wide cotton wadding
Scraps of fabric for the patches in pink, orange, red and patterned cotton
One skein each of six-stranded embroidery thread in Wedgwood blue,

Machine stitch all the thicknesses together $\frac{1}{8}$ in. away from the edge of the patchwork on the right side. Remove all the tacking stitches.

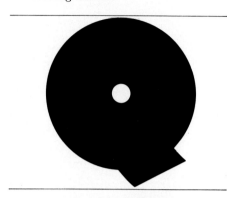

QUILTING

The origins of quilting are lost in antiquity, but are known to go back at least 6000 years. The word 'quilt' is derived from the Latin 'culcita', meaning a stuffed mattress or cushion, and a handicraft interpretation means the joining together of layers of fabric by tiny running stitches. In its earliest form, quilting was utilitarian, done for warmth and protection, and the stitches were purely functional for the purpose of securing a padding between two outer layers of fabric. As it developed over the centuries, the stitches were gradually used to form patterns so that the decorative aspect came to predominate. Inspiration for these patterns came from every-everyday objects found in nature – such as flowers, leaves, shells and feathers.

Although quilting has always, and is still, used in the making of clothes, it is mostly associated with the making of beautiful 'bed-quilts'. These came into common domestic use mainly during the fifteenth century and from that time onwards, women from all walks of life, turned their attention to the making of more and more elaborate quilts. The quilting frame was an essential item of equipment in most homes, and young girls were taught to use it at an early age. It is quilting such as this, worked by hand in a frame that is described below, and even though most modern quilting is worked with the aid of a sewing machine, thus dispensing with the need for a frame, the same principles apply.

How to Quilt
Tools and equipment:
Quilting Frame

Chairs or trestles on which the frame can be rested
Needles (No. 9 betweens)
Tacking cotton and No. 40 cotton
Large yarn needle
Piece of tailor's chalk
Several yards of tape
A 'top' either plain material or combination of patchwork, appliqué and plain material
Backing material
Filling or wadding
Fabrics: For the traditional type wadded quilt, where the sewn design is completely reversible, the top and backing should be of the same quality material. This should be smooth and soft, preferably with a sheen, but not shiny. Sateen, poplin, dull satin and silk are all good. If, however, the top is patchwork and/or appliquéd, then an inferior material, such as calico, can be used for the back-

ing, as the quilt will not be reversible. Avoid having a seam down the centre of the top. If two widths are needed, split one width down the middle and sew a half to each side of the centre panel.
Filling: The filling can be of well washed, carded sheep's wool, cotton wool or the modern polyester waddings.
Frame: the quilting frame (see diagram 1) consists of two long bars of wood called rails and two short pieces which are stretchers. The stretchers fit into slots in the rails and are held in place by wooden pegs fixed in holes. Occasionally the quilting frame rests on its own trestles, more usually it is rested on the tops of two straight-backed chairs. For a full sized quilt the frame should be at least 90 ins long. A frame 36 ins long is sufficient for making cot quilts and cushion covers.
A piece of webbing or braid is tacked to the inner edge of each of the rails.
For small pieces of work a large embroidery frame can be used, provided that it rests on a stand, as it is essential to have both hands free for the work.

Method of working
If you are making a big quilt all seams must be sewn and pressed flat and all appliqué and patchwork must be finished before quilting.
For a smaller item, the outline of the finished article should be marked on the top material before starting to work. It should not be cut out until the quilting has been completed as sometimes the work can twist slightly out of shape.

Patterns
In deciding which patterns to work, bear in mind the uses of the finished article. A cushion cover should have the principal emphasis in the centre, while on a bed quilt the centre pattern should fit the top of the bed.
Although in days gone by, an experienced quilter would seldom make sketches of the general plan, it would be helpful to do so. Remember that the sewing, in addition to being decorative, is used to hold the three layers together, so that the maximum unquilted spaces should be approximately 2 ins across.
If you are using templates to mark your patterns, they should be firm, and can be made of cardboard, metal or plastic. You can build up patterns from simple shapes or you may prefer to use some of the traditional ones (see pages 96 and 98). Whatever pattern or design you decide on, draw it out on paper before transferring it to the cardboard or metal from which the template is to be cut.

Marking
Having decided upon the patterns you want to use mark them out on the top of the fabric before setting it in the frame. Spread the top over a thick blanket on a table or on the floor. Mark the centre

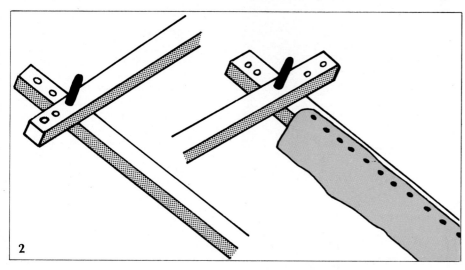

2

3

line and any other relevant points. Place the appropriate template in position and mark round it with a yarn needle holding it almost flat on the material so that it makes a slight crease in the surface. Mark any awkward patterns in tailor's chalk which is easily removed. On no account use pencil, as pencil marks are very difficult to wash out. If your pattern is based on parallel lines, these should run parallel to one another and when interrupted by another pattern they should continue on the other side just as if there had been no break.

As a rule the solid lines shown on a template are marked in, and the dotted lines sewn in freehand.

Framing up

When the pattern has been marked, set the work in the frame (see diagram 1, page 92). With the frame still in four separate pieces sew the backing material at both ends to the webbing which is attached to the rails. Roll the material round one rail until only 18 ins is left exposed. Fix the stretchers through the slots in the rails and insert the four pegs to keep them in place (see diagram 2). The work should not be too tight. The padding is then laid on. If you are using cotton wool or wadding warm it slightly to make it fluffy and lay it on to the backing carefully and evenly. The surplus should hang over the far rail. If you are using carded wool lay it on piece by piece to give an even thickness. You can only put on enough wool to cover the 18 ins width at any one time, so each time you have to roll on the quilt, you will need to add more wool.

Lay on the top with the pattern already marked to fit exactly. Tack it firmly along the side next to the front rail, making sure your tacking goes through all three layers (see diagram 3).

Fasten it along the far side with plenty of pins. The weight of the filling and top hanging over the far rail helps to keep the material taut.

Tie one end of the tape round a stretcher, close to the rail. Then take it across and pin it to the edge of the work, through the three layers. Loop it round the stretcher again, and pin to the work a few inches farther on. Continue in this way to the end (see diagram 4). Treat the other edge in the same way so that the work is firmly held. The quilting frame should be at a comfortable height for you to work. Work the quilting patterns with small even running stitches taken through all three layers of material. Use a fine cotton (not mercerized) or pure silk, to match the colour of the top fabric, and use a small fine needle. Regularity of stitch size is the most important thing in quilting. The most accurate way to work is to keep one hand beneath the work, and push the needle vertically down through the layers of

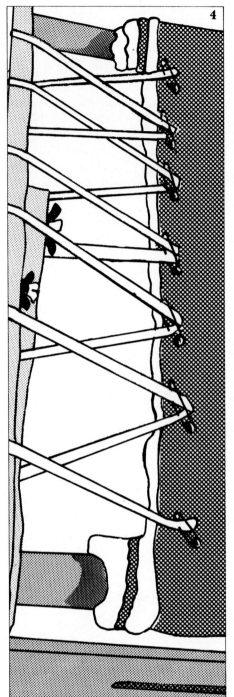

material from the top. Then push the needle back up through the work from the underneath to complete the stitch. It is a slow laborious business, and with more experience you will be able to take several stitches before pulling the needle away from the work. Draw knots at the beginning and end of the thread through to the wadding so they do not show on either side.

When you have quilted the portion of the work in the frame, take out the tapes and pins at the far side of the work, and carefully roll the sewn part round the near rail so exposing another length of the unsewn fabric. Fix this the same way as before. Repeat this procedure until you have worked all the quilting.

Finishing

There are various methods of finishing the edges.

When you have taken the quilt out of the frame, turn in the edges of the top and backing and work a line of running stitch as near to the edge as possible. (Make sure the padding does go right to the edge.) Then run a second row of stitching $\frac{1}{4}$ in. inside the first. For smaller items such as cushion covers and sometimes cot quilts, a piped edge is used. Use pre-shrunk piping cord, cover it and sew it on to the sides. On many American quilts the edge is bound. The backing material is cut initially slightly larger than the top, and when quilting is completed it is turned over the top and hemmed down. Alternatively the edges may be trimmed and bound with a bias strip cut in the same or matching material as the top (see diagram 5 A, B and C, opposite).

Forms of quilting

Trapunto or stuffed quilting: These are the same but the term Stuffed Quilting is more usual nowadays. Any good closely woven fabric can be used for the top but the backing must be of muslin or scrim or anything in a coarse weave that is not too thick. A small quantity of soft wool or cottonwool is needed for the stuffing. The pattern is marked out as in ordinary quilting and then worked in the usual way, although small back stitches may be worked instead of running stitches. When the outline has been worked and it has been decided which areas of the design are to be stuffed the backing is parted and small pieces of stuffing are inserted between the two layers (see diagram 6). A stuffing stick or any blunt instrument such as the end of a crochet hook will serve the purpose. When the area is fully, and quite tightly padded, the parted threads of the backing must be pulled together and secured.

Most of the traditional quilting patterns can be adapted for this technique, which is particularly good for adding emphasis to leaves and the petals of flowers.

Italian quilting: Italian quilting is worked on the same kind of fabrics as those suitable for Stuffed quilting.

The pattern is again worked as for any other type of quilting but this technique is really confined to lines, usually parallel lines, that should have as few breaks or intersections as possible. When the design is stitched, a cord, ideally thick soft wool known as Italian quilting wool, is threaded onto a tapestry needle and pulled through the channel made by the lines of stitching. When the lines cross or if there is an abrupt change of angle the wool must be pulled out and then re-inserted into the same hole. It is advisable to leave a small loop at these points (see diagrams 7 and 8), which will prevent puckering and allow for shrinkage.

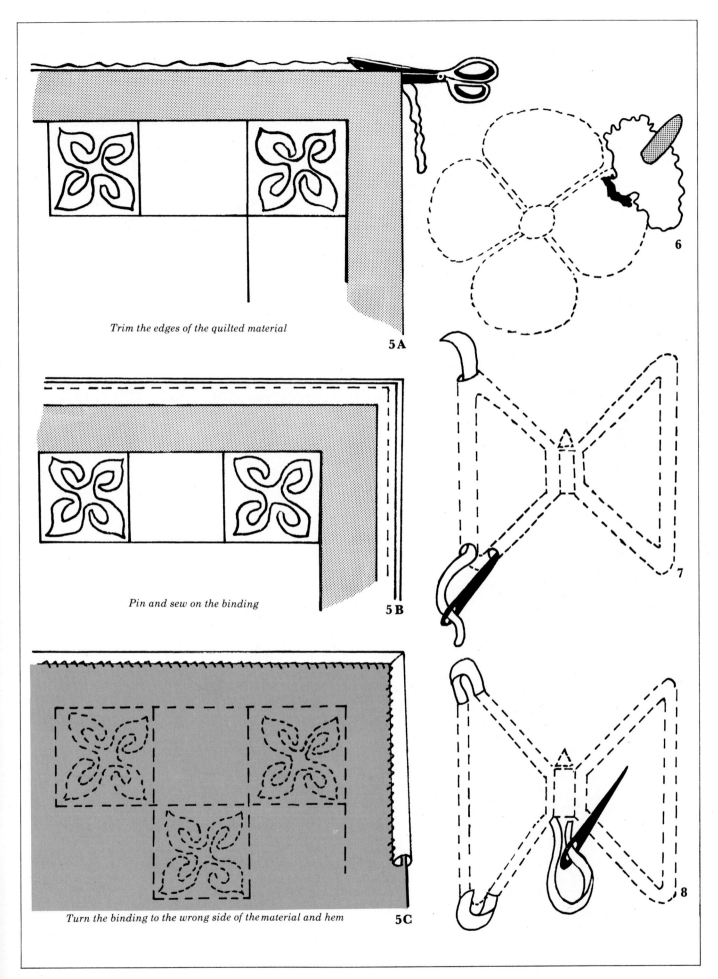

Trim the edges of the quilted material

5A

Pin and sew on the binding

5B

Turn the binding to the wrong side of the material and hem

5C

6

7

8

Contour quilting: This type of quilting is worked only on items which have applique designs on them. Rows of running stitches are worked about $\frac{1}{2}$ in. apart following the lines of the applique and giving the impression of contour lines on a map. The quilting is thus governed entirely by the overall design made by the appliques.

Other forms of quilting: There are other forms of quilting beyond the scope of this particular book, usually covered by the general term 'linen quilting'.

Linen quilting uses no wadding as an inner layer, as its purpose is solely for decoration and not for warmth. Here the sewing is often done in silk in back stitch and in monotone. Embroidery is sometimes incoporated into .the design. In the 17th and 18th Centuries, particularly, this form of quilting was used for men's waistcoats, jackets for children and head caps, as well as for coverlets and bed-hangings.

Quilting patterns

Below are some suggested patterns for quilting. The patterns are stitched straight on to the material being quilted and do not rely on the use of patchwork and appliqué for effect. In all cases the pattern outlines should be marked on to the material before quilting is begun.

Patterns based on circles: There are endless variations of patterns based on circles. Only 3 are illustrated i.e. Shell, Star and Rose, (see diagram 1, 2 and 3), but you will be able to think of many more. Draw a circle the size you require and mark the pattern to fit inside it. Many of these will look particularly effective if worked on to material which has a circular motif.

Patterns Based on Straight Lines (see diagrams 4 and 5). These lines are continued in a regular fashion all over the material being quilted.

Wineglass or teacup patterns: Wineglass or teacup patterns are produced by combining ordinary circles together in a

Right: *Quilted Flower Cushion.*

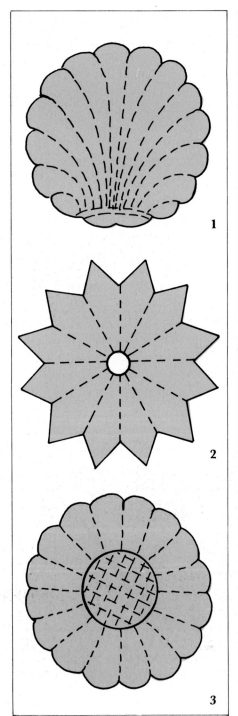

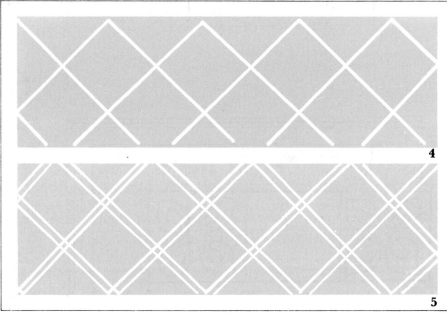

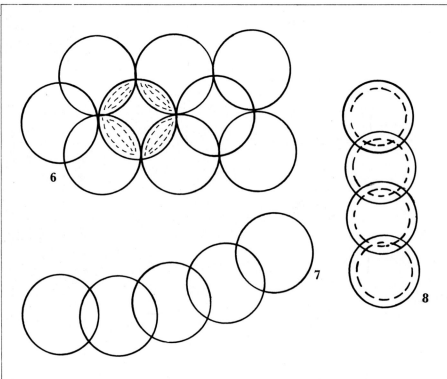

variety of ways (see 3 suggestions, diagrams 6, 7 and 8).

Miscellaneous designs: In addition to the more uniform designs, there are endless miscellaneous ones which can be used to make attractive quilting patterns. Use those given here as trace off patterns to make templates, (see diagram 9 – Welsh Tulip design, diagram 10 – Thistle design and diagram 11 – Paisley Pear). Mark the outlines only onto the fabric, and quilt along the dotted lines.

QUILTED FLOWER CUSHION

Materials

½ yd of 36 ins wide curtain fabric, printed with 2 bold flower designs
Matching sewing threads
Washable wadding 16 × 32 ins
Muslin 16 × 32 ins
Cushion filling

Method

Cut the curtain fabric into 2 pieces, each 18 × 18 ins with a flower design on each. Cut the muslin and wadding into 16-in. squares and tack the wadding to the wrong side of the curtain fabric, leaving a 1 in. margin all round. Tack the muslin on top of the wadding.

If quilting is to be done by hand, mount one side of the cushion in a frame, with the right side uppermost, and quilt round

Right: *Boy's Quilted Waistcoat*

1

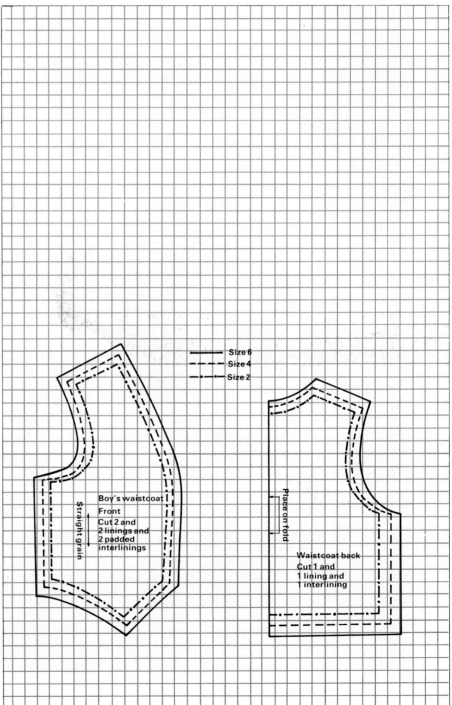

9

10

11

———— Size 6
– – – – Size 4
–·–·– Size 2

Straight grain

Boy's waistcoat
Front
Cut 2 and
2 linings and
2 padded
interlinings

Place on fold

Waistcoat back
Cut 1 and
1 lining and
1 interlining

the outlines made by the pattern (see diagram 1, page 98). Repeat on the other piece. Alternatively, stitch round the outlines using a sewing machine. Place the 2 sides of the cushion together, with right sides inside and machine stitch round the edges of the wadding, leaving an opening in one side. Trim the excess turnings and turn the cushion to the right side. Stuff it through the opening and then oversew the edges firmly and neatly. (Alternatively, you could machine round 3 sides only, turn the cushion to the right side, and insert a ready-made 16-in. cushion, before oversewing the fourth side.)

QUILTED WAISTCOAT

Materials
1½ yds of 36-in. wide (or 1⅛ yds of 45-in. wide) velvet, lining fabric and washable wadding
Matching thread
6 metal buttons
18-in. length of silk cord

Method
Using the graph pattern (page 98) make paper patterns of the waistcoat (see page 42, 5 squares = 4 ins.). Use these to cut out both pattern pieces in all 3 fabrics. Allow an extra inch all round the pattern pieces, and cut velvet with the pile running up towards the neck.
Place wadding under velvet (i.e. wadding on wrong side of velvet) and tack together. Using quilting foot and guide on the sewing machine, quilt velvet on the bias into 1-in. squares, making sure that lines match up the front. If your machine has no quilting foot, rule the sewing lines with tailor's chalk and sew with an ordinary straight stitch.
When you have completed the quilting, re-cut the front and back of the waistcoat to the right size. With right sides of velvet together stitch front to the back at side seams. Clip curves.
With right sides of the lining together stitch the side seams. Press under ⅝ in. on shoulder edges. With right sides together, pin facing to vest, keeping raw edges even. Stitch together all round except for the shoulder edges and a 6-in. opening in the stitching at the lower edge of back so the waistcoat can be turned the right way out. Trim all seams and corners. Clip curves. Turn waistcoat to the right side. Either use a special velvet board, or lightly press using a Turkish towel as a base. Slipstitch back edges together along the 6-in. break.
Sew shoulder seams of velvet with right sides facing. Press seams open. Turn under surplus and slipstitch shoulder edges of lining together.
Sew on buttons. Cut cord into 6-in. lengths. Working one at a time, sew ends of the cord under the buttons on the right hand side, making 3 loops (see diagram

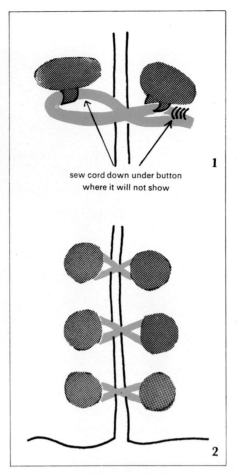

sew cord down under button where it will not show

1

2

1). These are then twisted once over the opening and looped round the left hand buttons for fastening (see diagram 2).

RIBBON CRAFT

Ribbons and braids are marvellous materials. The extremely wide variety of plain and patterned types available in endless colours and differing widths, gives enormous scope to their use. They can be used to add finishing touches to anything you make, and strong ribbons could be woven together to make attractive and unusual mats or wall hangings.

RIBBON AND BRAID MATS

Materials
For each mat:

Woven fabric, 9 × 12 ins. (½ yd of 36 in. wide fabric makes 6 mats)
½ yd of braid or ribbon

Method
Cut the fabric to size, (see under **Materials**), following the thread. Draw 3 or 4 threads about ⅝ in. from the edge, all the way round. Zig-zag the inner edge on the sewing machine – or hem-stitch, by hand – and then pull away the remaining outer parts to form a fringe.
Cut the ribbon or braid into strips to fit the mat, allowing ½ in. at each end to turn under. Pin or tack into position, making sure it is absolutely flat, then hem-stitch neatly all the way round.
The braids used for the mats illustrated are 1½ ins wide (silk embroidery on black ribbon), 1¼ ins (two-colour woven) and 1 in. (the different coloured embroidered daisies).

RUG MAKING

There are many different ways of making rugs – the most popular and successful of which is probably the 'hooked rug' method. This is a handicraft in its own right, which has been universally practised and enjoyed by men and women alike.
Before explaining in detail how to work hooked rugs, it is worth mentioning some of the other methods of rug making, not explained in detail in this book, but which you might like to explore further yourself. 'Rag Rugs' have become increasingly popular and are quick and easy to make. They are extremely economical, because, as their name suggests, they may be made from odds and ends of fabric left over from sewing handicrafts. Different effects in rag rug making may be achieved either by cutting the rags into small strips and hooking them into rug canvas, or by cutting them into long strips and weaving them over string or cotton yarn.
Another way of making rugs, particularly acceptable as bedroom rugs, is by crocheting them in thick wool. An example of this is given in our nursery rug (instructions given on page 108), which has a suitable motif worked on to it. This idea could be developed to suit any circumstances.

Hooked rugs
The most obvious advantages of hooked rugs are that the work grows very quickly and the end result is a thick luxurious pile rug that not only lasts a long time, but has cost far less than a bought rug of similar quality. Quickness of work can be further aided by two people working on it at the same time, starting

Right: *Ribbon and Braid Mats*

at either end. As long as the instructions described below for doing this are followed, the finished rug will look as if it has been made by one person, unlike such crafts as knitting and crochet, when it usually shows if another person has helped with the work.

Much the simplest method of making a hooked rug is to buy a kit. This already has the design printed on the canvas, and supplies the correct amounts of wool (already cut) in each colour, as well as a rug hook and full instructions for working the rug. If you prefer to be adventurous, however, you can buy plain rug canvas, use a charted design and make up the rug in your own colours (as you can do with the rugs that follow), or if you are really creative you can buy canvas and wool and make up a design of your own! This can be fun if you want a striped or abstract design, or something simple like a checkerboard effect, but if you have never made a rug before it is better to start with the kit or chart method.

Materials and equipment

Canvas: All hooked rugs are made on rug canvas, and there are various widths available from 12 ins to 48 ins. The canvas is whitish in colour and made of the best quality cotton, with a selvedge down both sides. It usually has nine holes to the square inch, with coloured lines (blue, red or brown) dividing up the canvas into squares.

Always buy the best canvas you can – the rug will last longer.

Kit canvases do not need line markings, because the design is printed directly on to the canvas so counting out the holes is unnecessary. Another reason why this is the best method for beginners! You will need a little more canvas than is required for the finished rug, because it is usual to turn over the canvas at both ends and work double for the first 5–6 rows. Allow an extra 6 to 9 ins for this (kits allow for this turnover). Circular, semi-circular and oval rugs are usually worked on square or rectangular canvas and cut to shape after the rug is hooked.

Wool: The correct wool to use for hooked rugs is a coarse 6-ply rug wool. This is available ready-cut and done up in round bundles or in skeins which can be cut to the required length.

Equipment: A rug hook or latch hook (see diagram 1), is the only tool you will need if you are using ready-cut wool. Kit manufacturers supply one hook with each rug-making pack, and they are also easily obtainable from local handicraft shops. If you are buying skeins of wool and cutting your own, then you will need the wooden gauge for even cutting (see diagram 2) and a sharp knife, razor blade in a holder, or a good pair of scissors. Alternatively

you could use an automatic cutter (see diagram 3). These are available from shops selling rug wool and canvas. You will also need a rug needle or crochet hook to finish the edges.

Method

Begin working by laying the canvas on a table or other flat surface with the printed side up (if you are using a kit) and with the full length stretching away from you. As canvas is usually rolled up to bring it home, the purpose of the exercise is to flatten as much of it as possible to make working easier. To help do this secure it with a heavy weight – such as a pile of books – at intervals. To prevent the cut ends from fraying, fold the end of the canvas over like a hem, right-sides together, for about 2 ins or for the marked amount on the rug kit (see diagram 4) exactly matching each

hole with the hole beneath. Crease the canvas sharply along the edge. It helps to tack the double thickness in position, or even to machine it. This 'hemmed' edge is worked with rug wool through the double thickness (see also diagram 4). Leave the outside edge of the canvas free and one square at either side next to the selvedge so they can be oversewn at the end. Start working the rug from left to right (or *vice versa* if you are left handed) and knot each square in the canvas with rug wool (instructions for this follow below). Keep working in parallel rows all the time. Do not be tempted to work patches of the pattern and then join them up, as this could give an uneven finish and it would be easy to miss odd squares.

Note: If 2 people are working on a rug at the same time from opposite ends of the canvas, crease and tack or machine

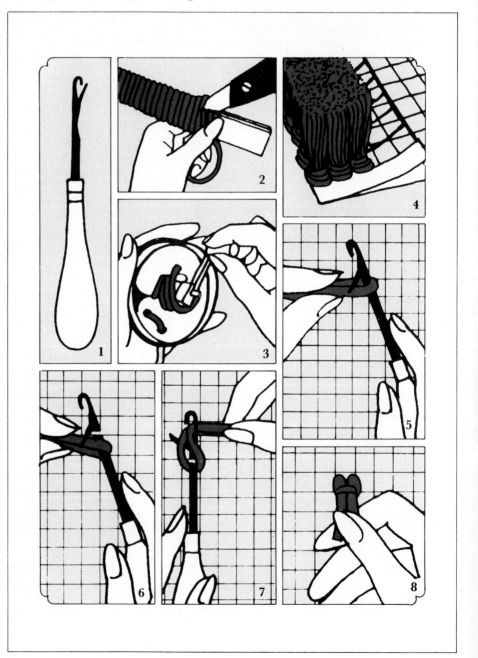

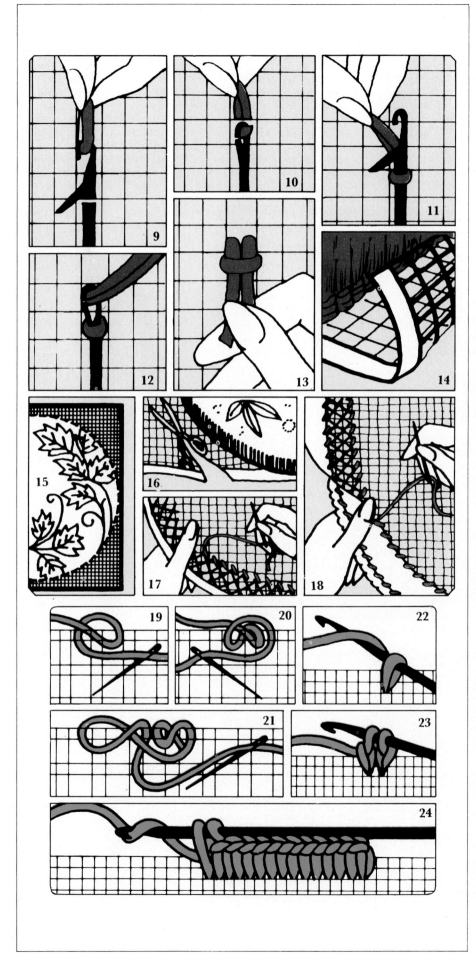

both ends before starting. One person should use rug knotting method 1 and the other method 2 (see below) so the pile lays in the same direction. They must both work to the same tension.

Knotting or hooking: There are 2 methods of working the knots in a hooked rug – the 4-movement method (see diagrams 5–8) and the 5-movement method (see diagrams 9–13).

The first method is quicker, but the difference in methods affects the direction of the pile. This is why it is essential to use only one method if you are starting at one end of the canvas and working straight through to the other end, or to use the 2 methods if 2 people are working from opposite ends.

Method 1, or the 4-movement method: Fold a cut length of wool in half, and hold it between the thumb and index finger of your left hand. Loop it round the neck of the latch hook, below the latchet (see diagram 5).

Still holding on to the ends of the wool, push the hook down through one square of the canvas and up through the one immediately in front (see diagram 6).

Put the two ends of the wool into the eye of the hook, turning the hook a little if necessary, and pull the hook back through the loop, giving it a flick upwards as you do so (see diagram 7).

Pull lightly on the 2 ends of the wool to tighten the knot (see diagram 8).

Method 2, or the 5-movement method: Push the latch hook under a double thread of canvas, until the latchet is through the canvas. Then catch the loop of a folded piece of wool in the hook (see diagram 9).

Pull the hook until the loop of wool comes under the canvas threads, holding on to the ends with your thumb and index finger (see diagram 10).

Push the hook and latchet back through the loop of wool and catch the hook round both ends of the wool held in the fingers (see diagram 11).

Pull the hook back, bringing the wool ends through the loop (see diagram 12). Pull lightly on the 2 ends of the wool to tighten the knot (see diagram 13).

If you are working with a rug kit, or a ready-stencilled pattern and cut wool, this is all you need to know to work your rug. When you start, work through the double thickness of the 'hem' and when you finish (if the rug is not being worked from both ends), stop about 10–12 rows from the end, (see diagram 14). Crease sharply as you did to begin working, and tack or stitch down. Then knot the wool through the double thickness of canvas.

Working from a chart: If you are designing your own rug, unless it is very simple as previously suggested, you will need to make and work from a chart. Alternatively you could buy a ready-designed chart or use one of the examples shown below. Each square on a chart represents a square on the canvas. Transfer the pattern from the chart to the canvas with felt pen. If the design is multi-coloured, then try to use a different felt pen for each colour, preferably in the same colour as the wool.

Fold the hem over first, then count the number of squares on the chart and mark them correspondingly on the canvas. Once you have transferred the complete design, you are ready to begin. Remember to work from selvedge to selvedge, completing one row at a time, and hooking each square, changing the wool colour as necessary. Again do *not* fill in bits of the pattern or work all of the areas in one colour first.

If you have designed your own rug pattern, by sketching it and painting in the colours, then the transferring of the design to the canvas is a little harder than working from a chart. Use squared paper to scale the design in inches, then transfer the design to graph paper so you can work out the knots per inch (3×3 holes = 1 square inch). Then transfer this to the canvas and work as above.

Quantities: With a kit, enough wool, rug canvas etc. are provided for the rug. If you buy a rug-making chart, instructions are given for the quantities of wool needed. If you are designing your own, a rug 72 ins long by 36 ins wide will take about $12\frac{1}{4}$ lb. of wool on coarse open rug canvas. A rug 54 ins long by 27 ins wide will take about 7 lb. As a rug obviously gets heavier as you work it, it is better to work on a flat surface pulling the work towards you as each row is finished. Support the worked end on your lap. When it gets too heavy, you can support the weight on a chair or stool, or turn the work round and work the second half from the other end. (If you do this, remember to use method 2 so all the pile lies in the same direction.)

Circular, semi-circular and oval rugs: If working from a kit or printed canvas, lay out the canvas on a table with selvedges to left and right (see diagram

15). Place weights – such as books – on the middle. Start with the short row nearest to you (see diagram 15), and knot one piece of wool into each square in the design using either of the knotting methods previously described. You must work from one selvedge towards the other, so you start with a short row which will have only a few knots, until you reach the centre of the rug where you will probably be working almost the full width of the canvas. Again complete each row before starting the next, knotting every square in the design, and never working in patches, or by individual colour. Naturally, you only work to the edge of the design and

not right the way across the canvas, and if you are working from a chart or your own design, mark the edge of the carpet before starting.

When you have knotted all the wool into the canvas, cut all round the canvas about 1½–2 ins from the edge of the design (see diagram 16). *Do not* do this before the design is complete. The canvas will fray and the design will either go out of shape or, you may be unable to complete the rug because the holes towards the edge will disappear as the canvas frays. Fold the spare canvas underneath the rug and stitch down securely using one stitch to each square of canvas (see diagram 17). Sew on

binding tape, so it covers the stitched-down edge of the canvas, using 2 rows of stitching, one stitch to each square of canvas, ⅛ in. from each edge of the binding tape as shown (see diagram 18). Binding tape is provided with kits when necessary.

Finishing touches

When the rug is completed, give it a good shake, then lightly brush the pile in one direction only, to remove loose fibres. Trim the pile lightly with a pair

Below: *left: Paisley Pattern Rug with pattern chart. Below: Geometric Design rug with pattern chart.*

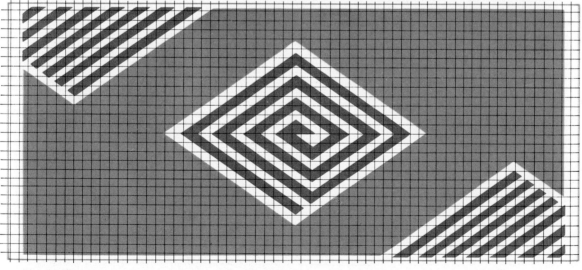

of sharp scissors. The 'hems' of the rug at either end should be firm but the selvedge edge is vastly improved if it is properly finished and strengthened. To finish the edges you will need skeins of rug wool to match the design.

There are two fairly basic edging stitches – plaited stitch and crochet edging stitch – which can be used to add the finishing touches. Either one would be perfectly suitable for most hooked rugs. Some people prefer to work the edging stitches first. This is a matter of personal taste, but it does mean you will avoid having to unpick any of the work due to miscalculations! You can work either edging stitch just on the selvedge edges, or if you prefer, all the way round the rug, in which case the 'hem' of the cut ends can be edged like the selvedge. To make doubly sure the end is firm, the first rows of tufts should still be knotted into double-thickness canvas. (It is usual to turn the raw edges of pile rugs over on to the right side, as previously mentioned.)

Plaited stitch: Work from right to left, using a rug needle. Turn the selvedge over so you only sew over half the width. With the right side of the work facing you, bring the needle through from the back of the canvas leaving about 3 ins of wool lying along the top edge of the work where it can be held in your left hand. This end of wool is covered by the stitches as you work along the canvas. Take the needle over the edge to the back of the canvas and bring it through again to the front, one hole to the left (see diagram 19, page 103).

Take the needle over the edge of the work and back through the first hole (see diagram 20, page 103).

Take the needle over the edge again and bring it through from the back to the front through the fourth hole along. Take it over the edge again as before and bring it back through the second hole to the right (see diagram 21, page 103).

Continue working along the selvedge in this way, moving forward 3 holes and back 2, passing the needle through from the back to the front of the canvas each time.

If you have not turned in a hem and the whole edge is to be worked this way, when you reach a corner, go back 2 holes, forward 2, back 1, forward 1 and then continue again with the first step.

Crochet edging stitch: Work from right to left and use a No. 6 (H/8) crochet hook. Fold over edge as for plaited stitch.

Push the crochet hook through the first hole and pull back a loop of wool leaving a piece hanging. (You can darn this into the back later.) With the loop still in the crochet hook, catch the wool from the back of the rug, over the top of the

canvas and pull it through the loop (see diagram 22, page 103).

Put the hook into the next hole and catch the wool from the back again and pull it through the hole. Then, catching the wool from over the top, pull it through the 2 loops already on the hook (see diagram 23, page 103).

Below: *Chart to show position of hedgehog and flower motif on rug. Colour key as follows:*

Key

× *Rust*

\ *Yellow (use two strands)*

● *Black*

Ⅳ *Stem Stitch (embroidered)*

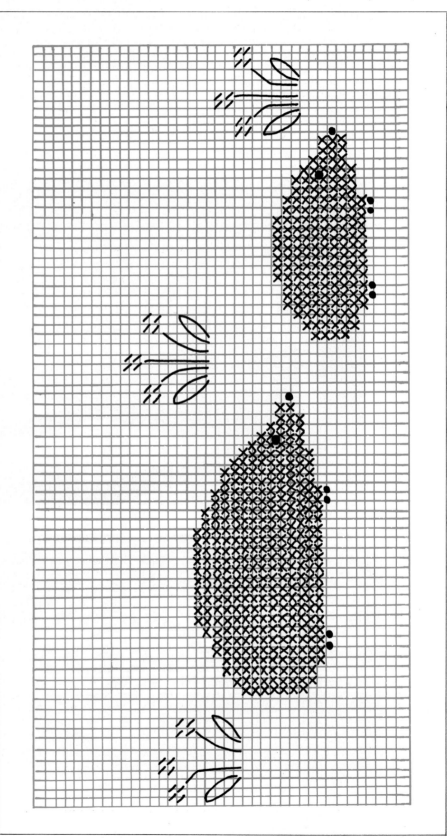

Right: *Crochet Rug.*

Push the hook through the third hole and continue in this way along the edge of the rug (see diagram 24, page 103). To join the wool, always leave a long end free at the start and end of a length of wool, to darn in afterwards.

Backing

Many people like to back their home-made rugs. Not only does this preserve the fabric of the rug and help to prolong its life, it also helps keep it clean. Hessian is a good backing material. Cut it slightly larger than the rug, turn in its raw edges and slipstitch it to the back of the rug. You can work extra stitching across the back of the rug to give additional firmness. These will be like large tacking stitches, but make sure they do not come through to the front of the rug or catch any of the tufts and pull them through to the back.

It is also possible to buy special non-slip backings, which can be sewn or stuck on – some are already adhesive, with a peel-off surface which is stuck to the back of the rug. This material can be purchased at handicraft shops and rug-making specialist shops.

PAISLEY PATTERN RUG

Materials

Rug canvas 27 × 58 ins
4½ lb. 6-ply rug wool or 36 packs of pre-cut wool in background colour
3 lb. 6-ply rug wool or 23½ packs of pre-cut wool in design colour
1 skein extra wool in background colour (for finishing edges)
Wooden gauge and knife, scissors or automatic cutter (if you are cutting wool)
Latch hook
Crochet hook or rug needle
(Finished size of rug: 27 × 54 ins)

Method

If you are cutting your own wool, cut a good quantity in both colours and keep them in separate boxes or bags.

To work from the chart (page 104), you can either plot each hole as you go along, or if you prefer, mark the design onto the canvas in felt pens. Fold the canvas each end to make a hem, then work in parallel rows from left to right, knotting wool into each square and changing the wool colour as necessary. (Follow previous working instructions.) When you have completed the knotting, work round the edges in plaited stitch or crochet edging stitch (see page 106) using the extra skein of background colour wool.

GEOMETRIC DESIGN RUG

Materials

Rug canvas 27 × 58 ins

4 lb. 6-ply rug wool or 31 packs of pre-cut wool in background colour
1½ lb. rug wool or 12 packs of pre-cut wool for dark stripe
1¼ lb. rug wool or 9½ packs of pre-cut wool for light stripe
1 skein extra wool in background colour (for finishing edges)
Wooden gauge and knife, scissors or automatic cutter (if you are cutting wool)
Latch hook
Crochet hook or rug needle
(Finished size of rug = 27 × 54 ins)

Method

Work in exactly the same way as for the Paisley rug and as previously described, following the chart (page 105), or first copying it onto the canvas. Finish the edges with plaited stitch or crochet edging stitch worked in the background colour.

CROCHET RUG

Materials

50 grm balls of Monsieur Pingouin (knitting worsted) yarn as follows:
4 in orange
2 in yellow
1 each in rust and green
Small amount of black double knitting (knitting worsted) yarn
No. 5 (H/8) crochet hook
Strip of felt 18 × 27 ins (optional)
(Finished size of rug = approximately 18 × 27 ins, excluding fringe)
Tension: 10 hlf tr. (h.d.c.) to 3 ins.
Abbreviations: see page 5.

Method

Using orange yarn, make 81 ch.
Foundation row: 1 hlf tr. (h.d.c.) into 3rd ch. from hook, 1 hlf tr. (h.d.c.) into each ch. to end.
Next row: 2 ch., 1 hlf tr. (h.d.c.) into each hlf tr. (h.d.c.) to end.
Rep. last row until work measures about 14½ ins. Fasten off.
To work the border: Turn and work in yellow yarn. Join yellow into last st. worked, 2 ch. for 1st hlf tr. (h.d.c.), 2 hlf tr. (h.d.c.) into same st., work 1 hlf tr. (h.d.c.) into each hlf tr. (h.d.c.) until 1 hlf tr. (h.d.c.) rems., 3 hlf tr. (h.d.c.) into last st. Now work 52 hlf tr. (h.d.c.) down left side of rug to foundation edge, work 3 hlf tr. (h.d.c.) into 1st ch. (at ch. edge) then work 1 hlf tr. (h.d.c.) into each ch. until 1 ch. rems., 3 hlf tr. (h.d.c.) into last ch., work 52 hlf tr. (h.d.c.) up right side of rug, sl.st. into 2nd ch.
2nd round: Sl. st. into next hlf tr. (h.d.c.), 2 ch., 2 hlf tr. (h.d.c.) into same st., work 1 hlf tr. (h.d.c.) into each hlf tr. (h.d.c.) and 3 hlf tr. (h.d.c.) into centre of 3 hlf tr. (h.d.c.) at rem. 3 corners, sl. st. into 2nd ch.
Rep. last round 3 times. Fasten off.

To work the tufted hedgehogs: First wind rust wool over a piece of stiff cardboard about 1½ ins wide. Cut at one side to make strands of wool about 3 ins long. Work from left to right from chart, using the colour key given. Insert hook under a hlf tr. (h.d.c.). Working in line with this hlf tr. (h.d.c.) from left to right, work a knotted loop by folding one strand of wool in half over hook and draw through a loop. Pass the 2 ends through the loop and tighten knot. Follow chart using 1 strand for hedgehogs, and use 2 strands together for dandelions. Using green single, work stalks and leaves in stem-stitch (see page 34). Using the black wool double, work nose, eyes and feet as shown in the photograph. Cut green yarn into 10-in. lengths and knot 2 strands through every alternate st. along short edges to make the fringe. Trim fringe. Oversew felt to back.

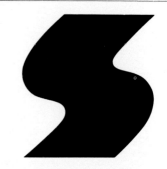

SMOCKING

Traditionally, smocking was a decorative needlework used on the centre front and sleeves of the 'smock' – probably the only garment which can truly be considered to be the National Costume of Great Britain. Apart from the smocking, smocks would have other symbolical embroidery on the collar, yoke and sides to show the occupation of the wearer. The art of smocking passed through an unfashionable period, when it was regarded as being somewhat rustic, and not delicate or elaborate enough for clothes of quality. Then it began to reappear as an integral part of children's clothes, usually on dresses, rompers and shirts. Still more recently, smocking has enjoyed a great revival of popularity and is now widely used as decoration on adult's clothes as well as children's. Literally, smocking is a 'kind of needlework used for holding gathers in place'. It is also extremely decorative.

How to Smock

Preparing the fabric: Smocking is worked with embroidery thread on the gathered fabric, and it is *essential* to prepare the fabric properly first. The gathers must be uniform, and are made in the ratio

2½ : 1, so allow 2½ in. of fabric for every 1 in. of finished work. If you are working with plain fabric you need to apply a smocking transfer first. These are sold with different widths, depths and spaces between the dots, so choose according to the size the finished work is to be. Press the fabric first, tack the transfer in position on the *wrong* side of the fabric and iron on with a warm iron, or a cool one if the fabric is very delicate or synthetic, then remove the paper.

Each individual dot *must* be picked up on the needle. Use a fine sewing needle and bright or contrasting coloured cotton, and as the running threads cannot be joined, use lengths of thread slightly longer than the width of the fabric. Knot at one end, then make a back stitch to prevent the knot from pulling through, and, working from right to left, put the needle in one side of every dot and bring it out on the other. Carry the thread to the next dot and continue in this way to the end of the row, taking care to put the needle in each side of the dot and not through the middle. When all the lines have been threaded with running thread, pull up the work carefully to the required width (with very deep gathers pull up a few at a time) and tie the loose ends to prevent the gathers from slipping. Even out the gathers. Although the gathers were made on the *wrong side* of the fabric, the smock-

ing is worked on the *right side*.

Fabrics with uniform dots, stripes and checks are particularly good to smock, as they can be gathered without the use of a transfer. If the design is not printed through to the wrong side, however, they will have to be gathered on the right side.

Basic rules: For the best finish, every gather should be picked up in the needle. Smocking stitches are usually worked from left to right with the exception of honeycomb smocking which is done from right to left. When working down, the thread must be *over* the needle. When working up, the thread is *below* the needle. For a top level stitch, the thread is *above* the needle. For a bottom level stitch the thread is *below* the needle.

Before starting to smock, plan the design carefully, maintain a sense of balance between the different types of stitches. Avoid monotony, and try to intersperse straight stitches with those which form a diamond pattern. Do not overcrowd the work – leave a blank line here and there. Also plan for an attractive blending of colours.

Fabrics: Almost any type of fabric can be smocked, but the lighter weight fabrics are the most successful, organdie, voile, lawn, fine cotton, poplin, silk, shantung and lingerie fabrics. Heavier weights can be smocked successfully such as linen, velvet and some fine wool

fabrics. Avoid textured fabrics as they do not gather well.

Thread: Stranded embroidery cotton is the usual thread used for smocking and it is split to make a thinner strand depending on the weight of fabric used. 4 strands are used for heavy fabric (wool, velvet, etc.), 3 strands for normal fabrics and 2 strands for light fabric (voile, organdie and fine lingerie fabrics). Linen can be smocked with linen thread and silk and shantung with silk thread. It is not wise to use wool as this is too heavy and breaks too easily.

Points to remember: The tension of smocking stitches will vary with each individual, but generally the finished smocking will be less wide than the pulled up gathers. When working the design, do not pull the smocking stitches too tightly or you will gradually close up the pleats. It is a good idea to practise a few stitches from the design you are planning to work, on a piece of gathered fabric beforehand. This will enable you to adjust your work if necessary. If the finished smocking is slightly too tight, you can remedy this by steaming the smocking and gently stretching it.

Always cut material for smocking with the selvedges at the side, never at the top and bottom, so that the pleats run down the fabric. If you are working with fabric that frays badly, machine stitch the raw edges, so that the frayed threads

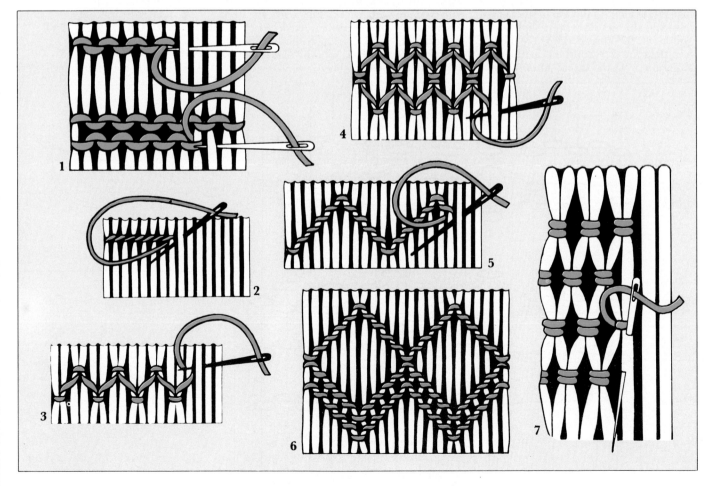

do not become entangled with the gathering or embroidery threads.

If you are smocking the back of a dress, start the design at the centre back, on one side of the back opening and work out to the side. Reverse the work and start the other side of the centre opening, working out towards the other side.

Smocking should never be ironed. After washing a smocked garment, pull the gathers firmly back into place while it is still damp, and if possible, dry flat, so the weight of water does not pull the work out of shape. If the smocking does become over-stretched with constant wear and washing, shape can be restored by stitching 2 or 3 rows of shirring elastic along the back of the pleats.

Basic smocking stitches

Cable stitch: This is a good, firm stitch, ideal for the top of a piece of smocking. Secure the thread at the left-hand side and bring the needle through to the left of first pleat on lower line; take a stitch through second pleat with the thread *above* the needle; take a stitch through the third pleat with the thread *below* the needle (see diagram 1, page 109). The lower section of diagram 1 shows two rows of cable stitch worked together.

Outline stitch: This is another firm stitch, simple to do, and suitable for the top or bottom of a piece of smocking.

Secure thread at left-hand side and bring the needle through to the left of first pleat. Pick up the top of next pleat, inserting the needle with a slight slope and with the thread *above* the needle (see diagram 2). Continue in this way along the row, the thread always above

the needle.

Outline stitch can also be worked keeping the thread always *below* the needle.

Diamond stitch: The first row in this stitch makes the top of the diamond (see diagram 3), and the second row completes it (see diagram 4). Either row can be incorporated into a pattern on its own. Secure the thread at left-hand side and bring the needle through to the left of first pleat on lower line; draw the needle horizontally through the second pleat with the thread *below* needle; with the thread still *below*, insert the needle horizontally through third pleat on upper line; with thread *above*, insert the needle horizontally through the fourth pleat on upper line; with the thread *above*, insert the needle through fifth pleat on lower line. Continue to end of row. Work the second row in reverse, immediately below the first one.

Trellis or wave stitch: This can be worked in single rows in a pattern, or in double rows, which again form a diamond shape. Secure thread at left-hand side and take a stitch through the second pleat on the same level with the thread *below* the needle; take a stitch in third, fourth and fifth pleats, each slightly higher than previous stitch and with thread *below* the needle in each case. Insert the needle horizontally through the sixth pleat with the thread *above* needle. This completes the upward slope. On the downward slope, work each stitch to correspond with the upward slope, but with the thread *above* the needle in each case (see diagram 5). Diagram 6 shows the second row worked in the reverse direction and also a third row worked

closely under the second row.

Honeycomb Stitch: If honeycomb stitch is the only smocking stitch to be used in a pattern, the fabric need only be gathered in a 2:1 ratio, as the stitch allows for greater expansion than usual. Unlike other stitches, it is worked from right to left and only a small stitch is seen on the surface. It is always worked in double rows.

Secure the thread to the right of the first pleat. Take a stitch through the top of the *second* and *first* pleats together and catch them together with a second stitch. Bring the needle down at the back of the *second* pleat to the second row missing out the first pleat on the right-hand edge. Catch together the *second* and *third* pleats with a stitch, then make a second stitch over the top. Take the needle back under work to the top line. Catch together the *third* and *fourth* pleats with 2 stitches, take the needle down at the back to the second row and catch together the *fourth* and *fifth* pleat. Continue this way, up and down, until the row is complete. Now work from right to left again on the second and third rows of gathering and so on until the smocking is as deep as required (see diagram 7). The thread, as in all smocking is *above* the needle for top level stitch and *below* the needle for bottom level stitch. Honeycomb can be worked from top to bottom, but most people find it easier to work from the bottom upwards.

CHILD'S SMOCKED SUN HAT

Materials
¼ yd of 36-ins wide cotton material with

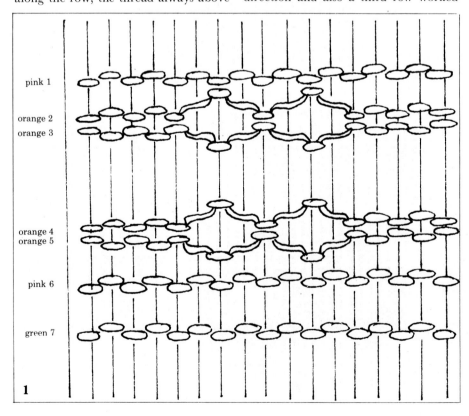

1

pink 1
orange 2
orange 3
orange 4
orange 5
pink 6
green 7

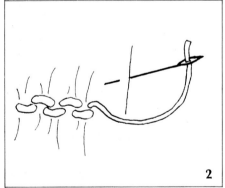

2

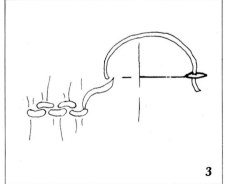

3

a firm weave
1 skein each of six-stranded embroidery thread in pink, orange and green
Transfer for smocking dots, $\frac{1}{4}$ in. apart

Method
Cut a rectangle of cotton material $4\frac{1}{2} \times 28$ ins. Cut a strip from the smocking dot transfer $1\frac{3}{4} \times 27$ ins and stamp it onto the wrong side of the material, 1 in. away from one of the long edges. Gather the rows of smocking as previously described and pull the gathers up so that they measure 10 ins.
Follow diagram 1 (page 110), to work the smocking.
Rows 1, 6 and 7 are worked in cable stitch, and rows 2, 3, 4 and 5 are worked in cable stitch and diamond stitch (see under *Basic smocking stitches* for how to work these stitches).
Use six strands of thread throughout and work the first line of smocking cable stitch in pink thread. Work the second and third rows in orange thread and

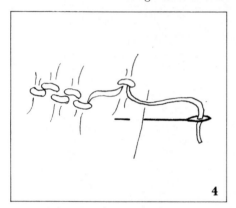

4

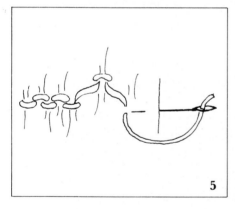

5

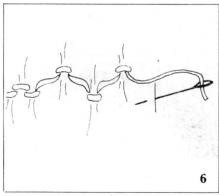

6

begin the second row with 5 stitches worked in cable stitch (see diagram 2). End with these stitches, with a stitch taken with the thread below the needle. Work 2 sets of diamond stitches (see diagrams 3, page 110 and 4, 5 and 6 left). Then work this pattern of 5 cable stitches and 2 sets of diamond stitches to the end of the row, ending with 5 cable stitches. Work the third row in the same way, but reverse the position of the thread, i.e. when it was under needle in row 2, it should be above needle in row 3, and vice versa.
Work rows 4 and 5 exactly the same as rows 2 and 3 in orange thread. Then work 2 rows of cable stitch in pink and green thread.
To make up the hat: Cut a strip of material 10×3 ins. With the right sides together, machine stitch this strip to the first row of gathers of the smocking, taking a $\frac{1}{2}$ in. seam. Fold the smocking and top strip in half lengthwise (right side inside) and stitch together $\frac{1}{2}$ in. from edge.
Machine stitch a $\frac{1}{4}$-in. hem along the edge of the piece of material with the smocking.
On the wrong side, gather the edge of the strip of material that you sewed on to the smocking, $\frac{1}{2}$ in. away from the edge, and draw up as tightly as possible. Secure the ends. (This is the top of the hat). Turn the hat to the right side.
Cut 2 strips of material 14×1 ins. Fold in half lengthwise, wrong sides together and stitch along the long edges, turning $\frac{1}{8}$ in. inside on both edges. Stitch the 2 ties to the inside of the hat half way between the back seam and front foldline.

SWISS DARNING

Swiss darning is an easy, but extremely effective way of introducing colour into items knitted in stocking stitch, without actually knitting it into the pattern. Although it looks as if it has been knitted in, it is added to the stocking stitch afterwards.
You can copy designs from any cross stitch or needlepoint chart or you can plan out your own motifs and borders on squared paper. If you do this, however, you should bear in mind that the stitch will be a little wider than it is long, so the final result will be contracted in length. This will not affect the appearance of a balanced Fair Isle or abstract pattern, but if you are using flower or figure motifs, they can appear rather squat and tend to look unattractive. In view of this, when planning charts for figures, animals and flowers, it helps to elongate the design a little, although it can be regulated easily enough during the working.

Method
Thread a large-eyed, blunt-pointed needle with the required yarn in the same thickness as the original work. Insert the needle into the base of the stitch to be covered, from the back of the work. Pass the needle behind the 2 threads forming the stitch and down again into the base of the stitch from the front of the work. Continue in this way until the stitches for the pattern have been covered in the correct colours (see diagram below).

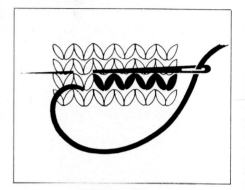

TIE DYEING

Tie-dyeing has been practised all over the world for centuries and it has proved impossible to trace its origin to one particular place. It is known to have existed in Japan from at least the sixth century, and China, from the seventh century. However, it is equally as indigenous to – and has been practised for centuries in – south-east Asia, Indonesia, India, Peru and parts of Africa.
Tie-dyeing, like batik (see page 13), works on a principle of 'resist dyeing', although the effects are achieved in quite a different way. A piece of fabric is folded, knotted, crumpled or twisted and then bound, tied and/or sewn in a variety of ways, so that when it is dipped into a dye bath, the colour penetrates only the untied areas. Patterns are made by the areas which have been partially or wholly protected from the dye and further effects and more complex designs can be achieved by re-tying and dyeing again in a different colour.

Fabrics

Natural fabrics, such as cotton are particularly good for tie-dyeing, as they respond to cold water dyes, and the colour produced is 'fast'. This ensures lasting patterns. Man-made fibre fabrics need a special dye, which generally is not as fast. Fabrics which have special finishes should not be used as, in general, they resist dyes. An exception can be made to this rule in the case of pure cotton with a special finish, on which cold dyes can be used. Even then, however, only strong colours of dye are suitable and they will still only give pale results. Wool fabrics can be dyed, but they sometimes lose their shape slightly.

Dyes

If you are using two or more dye colours, they will, of course, blend with each other. It is as well, therefore to keep the basic rules of colour mixture in mind:

Red + Yellow = Orange
Red + Blue = Purple
Yellow + Blue = Green
Purple + Green = Grey
Purple + Orange = Brown
Violet + Blue = Indigo

The following types of dye are widely available:

Cold dyes: Very easy to use in cold or warm water. For each colour, use 1 container for 6–8 ozs of dry fabric (approximately 2–3 sq. yds of medium weight fabric). For example, a 1 lb. dress for tie-dyeing in blue and red needs 2 containers of blue and 2 of red.

Multi-purpose dyes: Can be used in hot water. Simmering gives greater density of colour. For each colour, use 1 container for ½ lb. of dry fabric (2–3 sq. yds of medium weight fabric).

Liquid dyes: Convenient version of Multi-purpose dyes. It comes in a plastic bottle to dye up to 2 lbs. dry fabric (8–10 sq. yds medium weight fabric).

Use of dyes:

Cotton or linen: Either Cold, Multi-purpose or Liquid dye. Choose Cold dye for towels, sheets, pillowcases, tablecloths and anything else that is washed often.

Silk: Either Cold, Multi-purpose or Liquid (Multi-purpose and Liquid give richer shades on silk).

Rayon: Cold, Multi-purpose or Liquid.

Polyesters: Triple-strength Multi-purpose or Liquid.

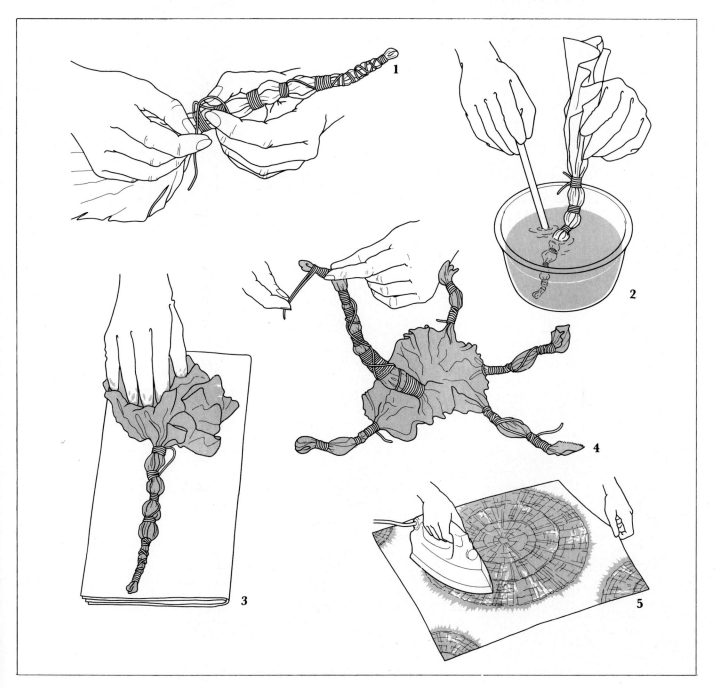

Polyester cotton mixtures: Cold, Multi-purpose or Liquid (use Cold for shirts and often-laundered items).

* If you want a strong colour effect, use more dye than recommended or leave the fabric in the dye bath for longer than is recommended.

How to tie-dye

The general instructions for tie-dyeing that follow, can be used with slight variations, for any article you plan to tie-dye. Although a particular technique (tied circles, using cold dye) is described, any other tying, folding or binding technique may be substituted. The actual dyeing and washing procedures will be the same. Also included are slightly varied instructions for Multi-purpose and Liquid dyes.

Cold or warm water method: Collect together the equipment you need. This includes a dye bath, which must be large enough to completely submerge the fabric. If you are using cold dyes, it may be made of metal, plastic, pottery or glass. In addition you will also need cold dyes, cold fix and household soda, rubber gloves, kitchen salt, a spoon for stirring the dye, a 1-pint jug and some thread, string, or elastic bands for binding the fabric.

Prepare the fabric to be dyed by washing and ironing it. If you are using cotton, boil it with soap powder to get rid of the finish that is usually present. If you want to achieve a soft effect in the dyed pattern, dry the fabric thoroughly before using it; if you want a crisper pattern, leave the fabric slightly damp.

Tie the fabric. For a circular pattern pull the fabric up towards the centre like a closed umbrella and bind downwards at intervals. Run the thread on from one solid band of binding to the next before knotting it finally (see diagram 1, page 113).

Prepare the dye, wearing rubber gloves. In general, use the lightest colour first.

Right: *Tie-dyed Pillow Case.*

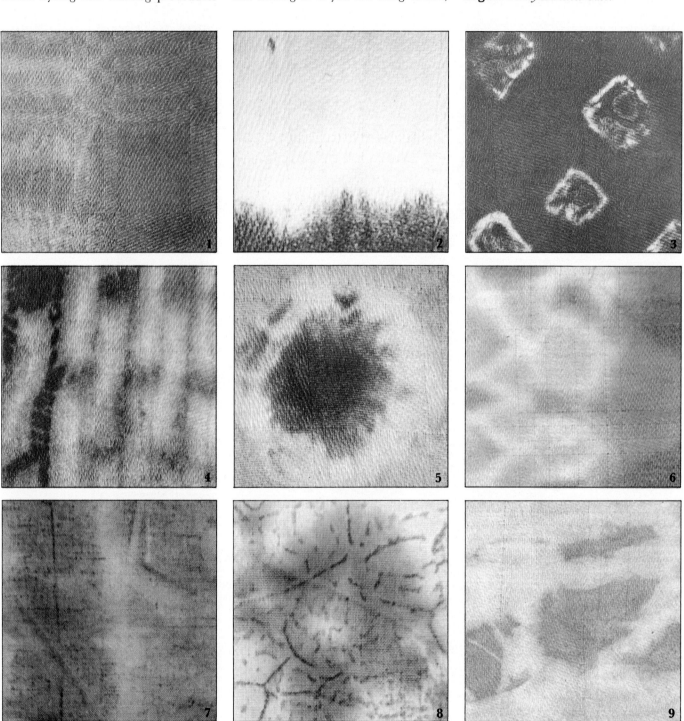

Pierce the container(s). Dissolve contents of each in 1 pint warm water and then dilute with cold water. Stir well and pour into the dyeing container. For each container of dye, dissolve 4 heaped tablespoons of salt in the dye solution. Dissolve 1 packet of Cold Fix (or 1 heaped tablespoon of household soda) in 1 pint of hot water. Stir well and add to the dye. Immerse the fabric for about 1 hour, stirring occasionally (see diagram 2, page 113). Remove from dye. Wash the fabric in boiling detergent solution, then rinse well until the water is clear. Dry out on folded newspaper (see diagram 3, page 113). (Thorough washing and rinsing removes all loose dye particles.)

When it is dry, untie the fabric. Re-tie it, adding central bindings, and also binding each corner (see diagram 4, page 113). Prepare the next dye bath and dye in exactly the same way as before. Then repeat the washing and drying procedures. Then, when the fabric is dry, untie and iron it (see diagram 5, page 113).

Hot Water Method: Prepare the fabric and collect the materials together in the same way as for the Cold or Warm Water Method, substituting Multi-purpose or Liquid Dyes for Cold Dyes and Cold Fix. If you want to simmer the fabric to get greater density of colour,

your dye bath container must be heat resistant.

Tie the fabric in the same way as for the Cold Water Method.

Dissolve powder in 1 pint boiling water, stirring well. Stir in 1 heaped tablespoon of salt for each container. Add this dye to the minimum amount of very hot water needed to cover the fabric. Immerse for 15–20 minutes, stirring occasionally, or, simmer over heat for 20 minutes.

Rinse until the water is clear and proceed with the dyeing, untying, re-tying, re-dyeing, drying and ironing

Right: *Tie-dyed Silk Scarf.*

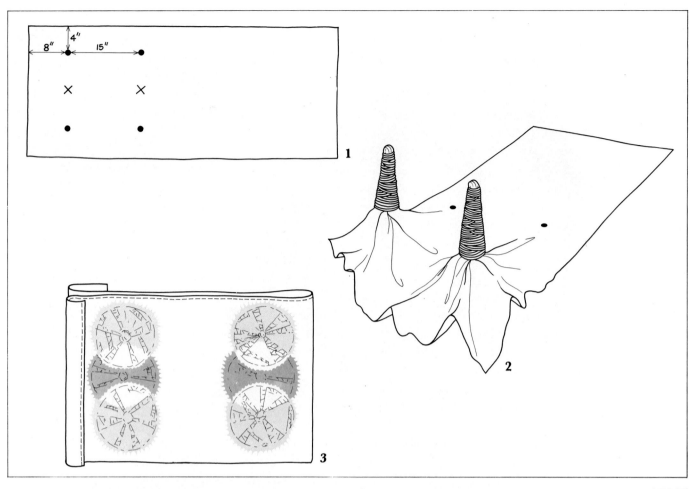

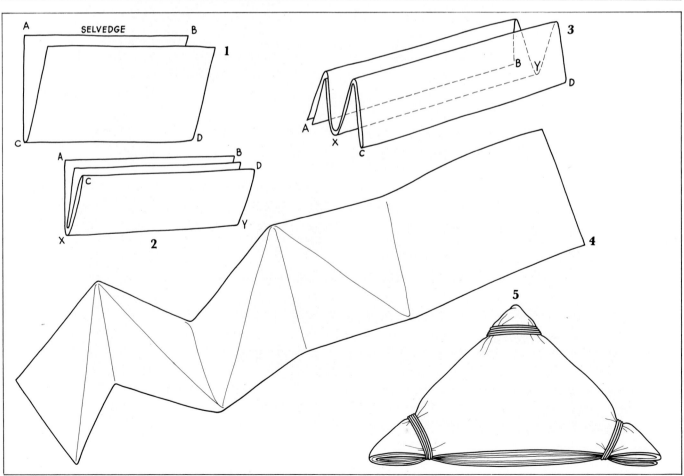

procedures as previously explained.

Other effects

Below are instructions for achieving 9 different effects with tie dyeing. They are just a few from the infinite number of patterns and combinations that can be worked. Each of these is illustrated on page 116 with corresponding photographs on page 114, and in most cases the instructions state the colour of dye used.

1. Fold the fabric and dip it into different colour dye baths (see diagram 1, page 116), allowing the colours to merge.
2. Fold the fabric and dip it into dye baths as above, but this time, avoid the colours merging (see diagram 2).
3. Tie a number of small stones into the fabric (see diagram 3). Dye yellow and then red.
4. This effect is achieved by concertina pleating the warp and weft of the fabric. Pleat the warp first (see diagram 4), and dye the fabric pale blue. Then pleat the weft and dye purple. Do not dry between immersions.
5. Tie pebbles into the fabric as shown in diagram 5. Keep this section out of the dye bath and immerse the rest of the cloth in yellow, then in pale blue. Finally dip the pebbled part in scarlet dye.
6. Fold the fabric as shown in diagram 6 and loosely tie it with heavy cord. Apply lemon and pale blue dye with a brush. Give a final applications of bright yellow dye in desired areas, using the brush.
7. Dye fabric rose pink all over. Then fold it in half (see diagram 7), and dip it in blue and light-brown dyes.
8. Crumple the cloth into a ball and tie it all over at random (see diagram 8). Dye in pink, pale blue and turquoise, re-crumpling and tying each time.
9. Fold the fabric into a strip and twist it, holding it at either end (see diagram 9). Dip the opposite ends into yellow and blue eyes.

PILLOW CASE

Materials

White cotton sheeting, 60 × 18 ins
Fine string
Cold water dyes in Bahama Blue and Lilac

Method

Mark 4 dots (see diagram 1, top left). Pull up some material from each dot in turn and wind string around it up to the top, from a position about 3½ ins below the dot. Tie very tightly at the base (see diagram 2). Dye in Bahama Blue following the method previously described. Wash off the surplus dye. Untie the first 4 ties. Working in between the 2 circles in each pair, pick up the 2 points marked X (see diagram 1), and wind as before to a depth of about 5 ins.

Dye in Lilac Dye, and then wash off the surplus dye. Untie. Leave the material to dry and then wash and iron it.

Turn in 1½ in. hem at either end of the sheeting. Fold it with right sides inside so that the 2 sets of circles are symmetrically placed on the front of the pillow case (see diagram 3). (It is not possible to give exact measurements here as materials shrink by varying amounts.) Machine stitch up either side, then turn the right way out and press.

SILK SCARF

Materials

1 yd of 36-ins width white silk
Fine string
Cold water dyes in Bahama Blue and French Navy

Method

Fold the silk square in two, bringing selvedges together (see diagram 1, below left). Fold C D on to A B (see diagram 2). Fold C D back towards X Y and then fold A B back towards X Y. This will result in a zigzag strip of silk about 4 ins wide (see diagram 3).

Fold the strip diagonally up and down (see diagram 4). This will give a fairly solid triangle, measuring approximately 6 × 4 × 4 ins.

Tie very tightly across the 3 corners (see diagram 5).

Dye in Bahama Blue. Then tie again, very tightly on top of the first ties, extending farther in each direction.

Dye in French Navy and wash off surplus dye. Untie all ties, dry and wash the silk and iron it while it is still wet. Hand roll and hem the edges of the scarf.

TOY MAKING

Soft or fluffy toys are essential possessions for every child, but they are usually extremely expensive to buy. Making them is easy, and extremely economical.

Patterns for all the toys included here are given on a 1 in. = 1 square grid. In toy making it is a good idea to paste the paper patterns onto thin card and use them as templates. You can then use them again, if required. The long arrows on the patterns indicate the straight grain of the fabric (if it has one) and they should run parallel with these threads on the fabric. If you are using fur fabric, cut it so that the pile runs down the toy.

Just about any fabric is suitable for toy making, but if you are using patterned fabric, an all-over pattern is generally more economical than a printed one that runs in one direction only. Unlike dressmaking, it is usually advisable to cut out each piece separately. Not only is this a more economical way to use the fabric as you can juggle the pieces around to fit more closely, but it also allows you to place pattern pieces wherever you want to fit in with the pattern on the fabric.

Allow ¼-in. turnings on fur, wool, cotton and plastic fabrics, and ⅛ in. on felt and suede which do not fray.

Kapok is the best all-purpose filling for toys. It is soft and light and easy to handle and gives a smooth appearance to the finished toy. Cut foam is suitable for filling fur fabric toys as the bumps do not show under the fur pile.

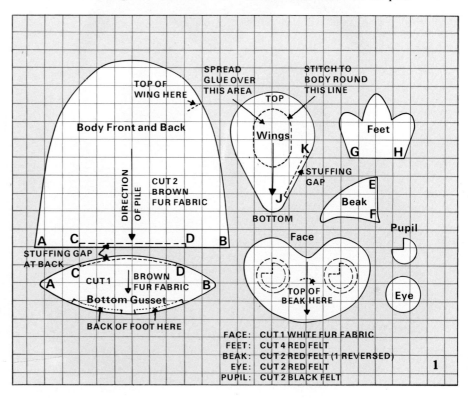

BACK OF FOOT HERE

FACE:	CUT 1 WHITE FUR FABRIC
FEET:	CUT 4 RED FELT
BEAK:	CUT 2 RED FELT (1 REVERSED)
EYE:	CUT 2 RED FELT
PUPIL:	CUT 2 BLACK FELT

FUR FABRIC OWL

Materials

Brown fur fabric, 15 × 24 ins
White fur fabric, 14 × 16 ins
Red felt, 12 ins square
Brown felt 2 × 4 ins
Matching threads
Kapok or other suitable filling (approx. 8 oz.)
Fabric adhesive
(The finished owl is approximately 9½ ins high and 11 ins wide.)

Method

Make and cut out templates for all pattern pieces (see diagram 1, page 119). Cut out all the pieces in felt and fur fabric (see instructions, diagram 1).
Body: With right sides facing, baste and stitch the front and back body pieces together from A round the top and down to B. Tack and stitch in the bottom gusset, matching AA and BB. Leave a gap open from C to D for turning and filling. Turn the owl to the right side and fill carefully so that the toy is a good shape but light and soft. Stitch the bottom gap to close it.
Face: Spread a little fabric adhesive on the eyes and pupils and stick them in position on the face as shown on the pattern. Oversew each piece neatly in place. Then spread a little adhesive all round the edges of the face and glue it onto the body in position. Oversew all round carefully, using small stitches. With the wrong sides facing, stitch both the beak pieces together ⅛ in. from the edge. Leave a gap open from E to F and carefully stuff the beak through this opening. Pin in position as indicated on the face and stitch all round very firmly.
Wings: With the right sides facing, baste and stitch the 2 wing sections together, leaving a gap open from J to K. Turn to the right side and insert enough filling to puff the wings out a little. Stitch the gap to close it. Spread a little adhesive on the inside of the wing and stitch it in place on the body as shown on the pattern. Take firm stitches, carefully picking up the body and wing fabrics alternately with the needle. Repeat for the other wing.
Feet: With wrong sides facing, stitch the 2 feet sections together ⅛ in. from the edge, leaving an opening from G to H. Apply a little adhesive along from G to H, and glue to the body in the position shown on the front seam of the bottom gusset. Stitch firmly in place and then repeat instructions for the other foot.
Using the eye end of a needle go over all fur fabric seams, picking out any fur pile that has become caught in the stitching. Brush the fur pile of the forehead downwards to fall over the edge of the white face piece. Brush over the rest of the owl to fluff up the pile, and plump him into shape.

HEDGEHOG

Materials

Beige felt 15 × 19 ins
Purple felt 6 × 11 ins
White felt 1½ × 2½ ins
Black felt 1 × 2 ins
Matching threads
Beige, cream and purple wool scraps (approx. 2 oz. in total)
Kapok or other filling (approx. 8 oz.)
Fabric adhesive
(The finished hedgehog is approximately 10 ins long and 5½ ins high).

Method

Make and cut out templates for all the pattern pieces (see diagram 2, right). Cut out all the pieces required in appropriate coloured felt (see instructions, diagram 2).
Body: With wrong sides of felt facing, stitch sides of body together from A, round the top and down to B. Stitch in

the bottom gusset on the right side, leaving a gap open from E to F for filling. Stuff until the hedgehog is a good firm shape, and then stitch up the gap.

Face: Spread a little fabric adhesive on the eyes and pupils and stick them in position as indicated. Oversew neatly all round each piece. Run a gathering thread all round the edges of the nose piece. Put a small piece of stuffing in the centre and draw up the threads. Stitch firmly to face at A, adding more stuffing to give a firm round shape.

Feet: Stitch 2 foot pieces together with wrong sides facing. Leave open from C to D. Insert a little stuffing to make the foot slightly rounded. Oversew gap and stitch foot to body in position shown. Repeat for other foot.

Spines: Cut the wool scraps into approx. 3¼ ins lengths. Take 3 strands together and fold in half (mix up the colours well). Stitch bundles at the fold to the sides and top of hedgehog until he is well covered (see illustration). Work as far as line G to H on the face.

Ears: Sew ears in position indicated on the head, curving them round slightly at the base.

Trim spines if necessary to make the

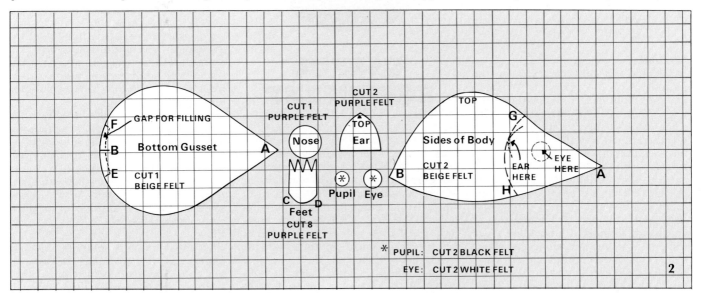

121

hedgehog well rounded, and brush off any excess filling.

RICE-FILLED FROG

Materials
Printed corduroy 9 × 15 ins
Plain corduroy 9 × 15 ins
11 oz rice
2 black beads
Strip of cardboard
(The finished frog is approximately 13 ins long and 7 ins wide.)

Method
Make and cut out templates for the pattern pieces (see diagram 3 below). Cut out both pieces required for the frog (see instructions, diagram 3). With right sides facing, stitch both pieces together round the entire frog, except for a gap from A to B to allow for turning. Clip carefully at curves and corners. Turn to the right side, pushing the feet well out to get a good shape. The blunt end of a pencil, used gently, will help you to do this. Bend the strip of cardboard to make a funnel and place the end of it into the filling gap. Pour in the rice. Stitch up the gap neatly.

Sew the bead eyes in position, as shown on the chart. Run a thread across inside the head from one bead to the other and draw up slightly, to 'sink' them into the head a little.

'Knead' over the frog, making sure that the rice filling will slide in and out of the legs freely.

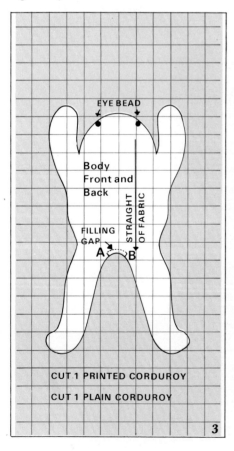

EYE BEAD

Body
Front and
Back

STRAIGHT OF FABRIC

FILLING
GAP
A   B

CUT 1 PRINTED CORDUROY

CUT 1 PLAIN CORDUROY

3

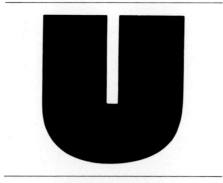

USEFUL EQUIPMENT

For all home handicraft work, you will always need a certain amount of basic equipment. Some tools are essential, while others help to make work easier. When buying sewing or handicraft equipment, it is a good idea to buy that of good quality, which is more likely to last and do its job efficiently. Before you begin to make anything, always check that you have all the equipment you are going to need assembled together. A selection of useful equipment is shown in the illustration (right).

Scissors
You should have a selection of scissors as different ones are needed for different things.

Embroidery scissors: (2 pairs shown on extreme left). Usually about 4 ins long with very sharp points. They are useful for cutting threads in embroidery work, and also for clipping into seams in sewing and for cutting buttonholes.

Trimming scissors: (3rd from left). Usually about 6 ins long, with fairly sharp points. They are useful for trimming seams after they have been sewn.

Paper scissors: (4th from left). Keep a pair of ordinary scissors just for cutting out paper patterns. These should be fairly large, to allow you to cut long stretches of paper at one time. Never use your dressmaker's scissors for cutting paper. It will blunt them very quickly.

Dressmaker's scissors: (medium and large pair illustrated on right). The most accurate kind of scissors for cutting fabric are the bent handled type, as illustrated. If you put your thumb in the rounded ring, the lower blade will rest flat on the cutting surface, ensuring a smoother, more accurate cut. To keep these scissors in good working order, lubricate the joint with a drop of oil each month and keep it free from fabric fluff. Never try to sharpen the blades yourself.

Pinking shears: (illustrated below dressmaker's scissors). Excellent to use as a quick and easy way of neatening seams and hem edges, or to give decorative edges to an applique motif for example.

They should never be used to cut out patterns as the zig zag edges cause innaccuracy.

Dressmaker's squared paper
(illustrated 2nd row, left). Comes in sheets measuring 30 × 20 ins and is marked into 1 in., $\frac{1}{2}$ in. and $\frac{1}{4}$ in. squares. It is extremely helpful in drafting pattern pieces from graph charts.

Needles
(illustrated in packets on dressmaker's paper). Hand sewing needles range from size 1 (coarsest) to size 10 (finest) and are available in several different types:

Sharps: medium length needles with round eyes for all purpose use.

Betweens: short needles with round eyes for fine sewing.

Millinery: long, slender needles with round eyes and used often in hand sewing for basting, gathering and shirring.

Crewel: medium length needles with oblong eyes used for embroidery.

Wool or darning: thick needles with blunt points and large eyes. As the name suggests, used for darning or woollen embroidery work.

Pins
(illustrated on dressmaker's squared paper). Use fine steel pins as these will not rust. The glass headed pins (illustrated on the left) are particularly good, as they are very sharp, easier to pick up and show up on most fabric backgrounds.

Pin cushion: (illustrated on right of dressmaker's squared paper). Useful to keep close by while working, with a selection of pins and needles stuck into it.

Threader: (below pin cushion) A useful gadget for threading a fine-eyed needle.

A quick unpicking gadget
(illustrated on top of glass-headed pins). Not essential, but a great help in unpicking seams when necessary, and also for taking out tacking threads quickly.

Sewing machine needles
(illustrated 2nd row, centre). Presupposes the possession of a sewing machine, which is also a fairly essential piece of equipment for home handicraft work! Keep a selection of needles to fit your machine which will be suitable for sewing different types of fabric.

Tailor's chalk
(illustrated right of sewing machine needles and left of pinking shears). This is available in pencil form or in blocks and is useful for marking pattern details onto fabric. Keep light and dark colours and use according to fabric colour so that they will show up. (Never use lead pencil on fabrics, it will not rub off.)

Thimble
(illustrated centre). A one-time essential piece of sewing equipment, but no longer used so frequently. It is worn on the middle finger of the sewing hand and is used to push the needle through the fabric. It will save wear and tear on the finger, and, once you are used to wearing

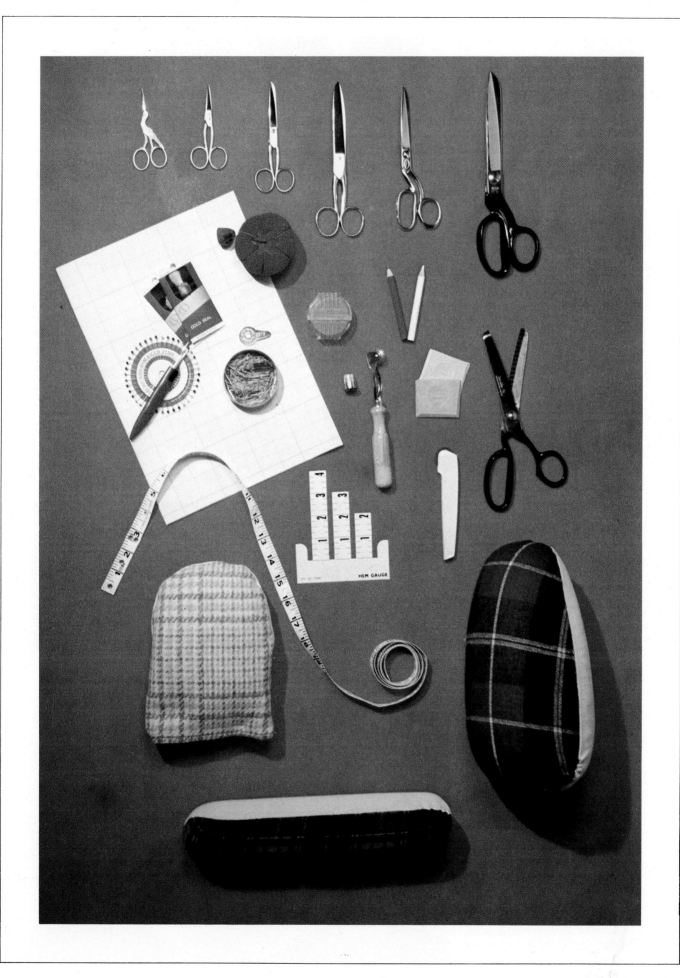

it, it will also save time. One with a steel lining will last the longest.

Tracing wheel
(illustrated, right of thimble and below tailor's chalk). Used for marking fabric in conjunction with dressmaker's carbon paper (see page 43). Choose one with sharp steel points.

Tape measure
An essential piece of equipment, they are usually 60 ins long, and should be marked in inches and centimetres. Those made of glass fibre with metal ends are the most satisfactory, and will not tear or stretch.

Hem gauge
(illustrated right and above tape measure). Again not an essential piece of equipment, but useful to check hems and turnings are a uniform width all along.

Pressing equipment
(illustrated at bottom of page). Shown here are:
Pressing mitt: (left) which is useful for pressing rounded areas of articles.
Tailor's ham: (right) which is slightly egg-shaped and useful for pressing darts. The surface must be completely smooth and the ham – very firm, to be effective.
Seam roll: (bottom), which is made by padding a short piece of wood with wadding and fabric, and is useful as an additional aid when pressing seams. None of these are vitally essential pieces of equipment, but they undoubtedly help to give a better finish. In addition, you will certainly need an iron (a steam one is the most useful), and an ironing board. A small sleeve ironing board can also be an asset.

Sewing threads
Not illustrated, but essential equipment for all home handicraft workers.
Mercerized cotton thread: used for all fabrics made from natural fibres such as cotton, linen, silk and wool.
All-purpose synthetic threads: which can be made of nylon, polyester or cotton-covered polyester and are recommended for sewing knitted and synthetic fabrics where elasticity and strength are important.
Silk thread: which is an alternative, and very good thread for sewing natural fabrics, particularly silk and velvet. Not always easy to obtain, it is also more expensive than other thread.
Buttonhole twist: which is a strong silk thread used for handworked buttonholes and sewing on buttons. Its thickness also makes it excellent for decorative top stitching.
Keep a selection of colours of all these threads so that you have them whenever you need them.
There are many kinds of other threads available for all sorts of embroidery and canvas work. Unless you do a lot of this kind of handicraft however, it is probably advisable to purchase the specific types as you need them.

VARIETY

Variety in handicraft work can be demonstrated by the number of different ways the same basic item may be made. A simple cushion cover for example, may be simply sewn in a fabric to match the décor of the room. But it may also be knitted or crocheted or embroidered in a hundred different ways: it may be pieced together in patchwork patterns; finished with quilting or applique motifs or made of fabric that has first been tie-dyed or batiked; it may be trimmed with ribbon or braid, or finished with tassels or fringing. It may even be woven.
We give instructions for making a basic cushion, which may be adapted to any size or shape.

ROSEBUD CUSHION

Materials
2 squares of check gingham, each 14 ins
1½ yds of 1 in. deep cotton fringe
Embroidered rosebud motifs
2 squares of fine cotton for the inner cushion, each 14 ins
Filling

Method
Cut the fabric to size (see **Materials**) and stitch the fringe to the right side of one piece ½ in. in from the edge, with the outer edge of the fringe towards the centre of the cushion. Stitch the rosebud motifs into position on the front of the cushion. With right sides facing, join the front and back of the cushion on 3 sides following the stitching line of the fringe. Trim seams, clip corners and turn to the right side.
Make up the inner cushion in the same way, omitting the fringe and decoration. Stuff firmly, then turn in raw edges and slip-stitch together. Fit inner cushion inside the cover, turn in the edges of the remaining side, and slip-stitch neatly. Alternatively, insert a zip or touch-and-close fastening, so that the cover can be removed more easily for washing purposes.

Right: *Nursery Wall Panel.*

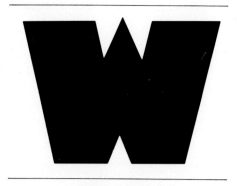

WALL HANGINGS

Wall hangings, like mobiles, have become increasingly popular in recent years. Dispensing as they do, with the need for costly picture framing, they provide an economical and bright answer for cheering up a large expanse of blank wall. Fun and creative to make, they may be as large or small as you like.

As with so many other things, wall hangings may be made of all sorts of materials. You can appliqué complete pictures using an assortment of fabrics or embroider a needle-point design onto a canvas background. You can work a bold geometric patchwork design or use tie-dyed, batiked or fabric-painted panels, depending on the circumstances of the room. They are particularly good accessories for a nursery or child's room, and the simplicity, economy and enjoyment attached to their making means they can be replaced as often as you feel the inclination!

NURSERY WALL PANEL

Materials
Orange evenweave furnishing [upholstery] fabric, 16 × 22 ins
$\frac{1}{2}$ yd of $\frac{1}{2}$ in. diameter dowel wood
Scraps of felt in dark and pale green; blue; pale, medium and dark pink; red; turquoise; fawn; pale lemon; white; purple; black; mauve/pink;

Left: *Pattern for Wall Panel*

a	*Pale Green Felt*
b	*Dark Green Felt*
c	*Blue Felt*
d	*Pale Pink Felt*
e	*Medium Pink Felt*
f	*Dark Pink Felt*
g	*Red Felt*
h	*Turquoise Felt*
i	*Fawn Felt*
k	*Pale Lemon Felt*
l	*White Felt*
m	*Purple Felt*
n	*Black Felt*
o	*Mauve/Pink Felt*
p	*Orange Felt*

yellow and orange
Blue cotton thread
Black and blue six-stranded embroidery thread

Method
Enlarge the diagram opposite and transfer to tracing paper (see page 42 – 1 square = 1 in.). Where one piece of felt overlaps another, trace the piece on top and the piece underneath and complete the overlapping lines.

Transfer the design on to the material, $2\frac{3}{4}$ ins away from the side edges and 2 ins away from the bottom edge, by putting a piece of carbon paper face down on the right side of the material and drawing over the lines of the design with a pencil (see page 43).

Following the diagram and using the tracing pattern, cut out all the pattern pieces from the appropriate coloured felt. Place them on the fabric and tack and machine stitch them in place.

Work rows of backstitch for the antennae, pixie's mouth and hat tassel with 3 strands of black stranded cotton.

Work French knots (see page 74), at the ends of the antennae and on the caterpillar's eyes, with 6 strands of black embroidery thread. Work the pixie's eyes in satin stitch (see page 34) with 6 strands of blue embroidery thread.

Make a 1 in. deep hem at the top of the wall hanging. Fray the fabric for 1 in. along the bottom edge and $\frac{1}{2}$ in. along each side. Thread the dowel through the hem at the top and tie a 21 ins length of cord either end of the dowel wood to hang the picture.

ZIG ZAG STITCH

Most modern sewing machines are equipped with a 'swing needle' which means they can work a zig zag stitch. This stitch can be used in a variety of ways and is an invaluable asset in sewing handicrafts.

Seams and hems
Use zig zag stitch to neaten seams on home-made clothes, providing the fabric you are working with does not fray too badly. Stitch along the seam turning in zig zag stitch and then trim the fabric close to the stitching, being very careful not to clip through it. You can also use zig zag stitch in a similar way round the bottom of hems on thick, but firmly woven fabrics, before turning them up. Stitch a row of zig zag stitch round the bottom of the hem, then turn it up and catch your hemming stitches to the machine stitches. Thus you do not have to turn under a double thickness of fabric.

Fabric use
If fabric frays very badly, zig zag stitch round the edge of all the pattern pieces before you sew them together. This will help to check the fraying as you work. Zig zag stitch is also good for sewing knit fabrics, as although it is firm, it allows a little more 'give' than straight stitching.

Buttonholes
Buttonholes can be worked in zig zag stitch. Set the stitches on the machine very close together, mark out the buttonhole area and then zig zag stitch along either side of it. Cut the buttonhole after you have secured the ends of the thread, being careful not to snip the stitches.

Gathers
A quick way of making neat gathers on skirts and sleeve heads is to use zig zag stitch. Set the machine to work a fairly wide zig zag stitch, then cut 2 lengths of strong thread the same length as the area to be gathered. Run this under the machine foot as you sew the zig zag stitch (see diagram 1). The stitching then holds the cord in place, and when you have completed the stitching, pull either end of the cord to gather fabric.

Decorative uses
Zig zag stitch has a variety of decorative uses in embroidery and applique work. Indeed, complete designs can be worked in zig zag stitch alone, or you can use it to fill in details on an overall design. If you are using it in applique work, first sew on the applique with normal straight stitch. Trim the edges and then sew round with fairly closely set zig zag stitches. Use machine embroidery twist for the most effective results. (Tracing or embroidery paper put under fine fabrics while machining gives 'body' to stitches and stops fabric from pulling.)

INDEX

Acknowledgments

Candles (photograph, page 23); candle-making and batik kits (photograph, pages 2–3) from David Constable, Candle Makers Supplies, 4 Beaconsfield Terrace Road, London.

Basketwork hamper (photograph, pages 2–3) from the Neal Street Shop, London.

Sewing, needlework and knitting materials (photograph, pages 2–3) from John Lewis Partnership, London.

Photograph, pages 2–3, by Dick Polak.